THEJAILHOUSE FINANCIAL PLAYBOOK

SAM FERRARO

Foreword by D.T. HOLT

THE
PRISONER PRESS
PRESENTS

THE PRISONER
PRESS
100 South Belcher Road
Suite 6053
Clearwater, FL 33758
www.theprisonerpress.com
Copyright 2025 by Sam Ferraro
Cover Design by 100covers.com
Send comments, reviews, and all other inquiries to:
info@theprisoner.com

First Edition : October 2025
ISBNs: 000-0-000-00000-0 (paperback): 000-0-000-00000-0 (eBook)

Library of Congress Control Number
Printed in the United States of America:

MISSION STATEMENT

It is the mission of the prisoner press company to provide a multimedia platform to help incarcerated individuals by providing them with information and resources they may need in order to make their time while incarcerated as productive and meaningful as possible, as well as achieve success once they are paroled and/or released back into the community.

Prisoner Press supports the right to free expression and the value of copyright. The purpose of copyright is to encourage writers to produce the creative works that enrich our culture.

DEDICATION

To My Amazing Parents:

Despite all the shit I've put you through - and it's been an epic proportion of shit you've never given up on me, even after everyone else in my life did. This book is proof of your support. Without you, none of what I've been able to accomplish would ever have been possible. There isn't enough money in the world to repay you for everything you've done for me. But, maybe, knowing I've finally found success in my life and have a promising future ahead of me is a good start.

Thank you, Mom and Dad.
I love you both so much.

TABLE OF CONTENTS

Part TWO

Principles Of Protecting Your Money from Prison Course

FORWARD

Forward

By D.T. Holt

I still remember the first time I met Sam. We were, as you can imagine, in prison. Actually, we were on a block specifically for inmates with a history of substance abuse. It was a drug treatment program, and neither he nor I really wanted to be there. But, whether we liked it or not, we'd reached the end of the road, and we knew it was probably our last chance to turn our lives around.

I was already in the program when Sam got there, and my first impression of him was of a guy exasperated with life. On their first day, the new guys had to stand up in front of the group to introduce themselves. It was a formality, and I usually wasn't too interested in learning about the new guys, so most of the time, I didn't pay too much attention during these "getting to know you" sessions. I'd sit slumped in my chair, letting my mind wander to all the places I'd rather be. But when Sam walked up there, I got a strange feeling that here was a person with depth. I don't know if you've ever had a gut instinct about somebody before - the sense that there was more to them than met the eye - but I sometimes do, and I definitely got that feeling looking at Sam.

Honestly, I don't know why because there wasn't anything especially noteworthy in his appearance. He was tall, heavy shouldered, tattooed; he looked like he might've played football in a former life. But there was something else to him, something in the way his eyes calmly scanned the room that suggested a level of intelligence that was out of place in that setting.

Later that evening, I saw Sam sitting alone in the dayroom reading a book. If you're familiar with the normal activity that goes on in a prison dayroom, then you know it's pretty uncommon to see a guy off on his own, utterly absorbed in a piece of literature. Prison dayrooms are loud, rambunctious places. Tables are filled with rowdy inmates hollering during games of cards or Dominos, trash-talking over games of speed chess, and guys arguing with one another to get next on the phones.

But not Sam. He seemed to have consciously removed himself from the fray, as if he had no desire to engage in the narrow-minded squabbling of his peers. His book- whatever it was - held his attention completely.

To tell you the truth, I felt a little bad about interrupting his reading to introduce myself.

What are you reading," I asked, trying to sound friendly. Without saying anything, Sam held up the book's cover for me to see. It was called Hyperfocus by Chris Bailey. Ironic, I thought, because he certainly seemed hyper focused on reading it. After flashing me the cover, he opened back to his page and picked up right where he'd left off. My presence, clearly, was unwanted.

But I would not be deterred. "What's it about?"

Sam sighed. "It's about how to ignore distractions," looking at me pointedly. I nodded. "Ah, I see. Yes, there are a lot of those in this place."

He went back to reading, no doubt hoping I'd gotten the message. But I hadn't. "So...where are you from?"

Sam snapped his book shut and gave me a long, steady look. The thought occurred to me that he might take a swing at me. And I think the thought occurred to him, too. But then, something in his expression seemed to soften. Sam relented.

3

And just like that, we spent the rest of the evening in the dayroom chatting about life.

My gut was right. He was a pretty deep guy.

Sam and I would become close in the weeks and months that followed. I would learn that, like me, Sam was a writer. We both spent countless hours toiling over our respective manuscripts and many times, we would meet up in the dayroom to exchange our work with one another for proofreading. I would confidently hand Sam pages and pages of rough drafts, certain that once he read them, he'd tell me I was a genius. But, no, he never did. Actually, to be honest, it soon became clear that Sam's greatest pleasure in life was criticizing my writing style. He'd tell me I sounded too self-conscious, that I was trying too hard, and that I was a stuck-up douchebag.

As a retaliation, I soon reciprocated the gesture. When Sam would hand me his rough drafts, beaming with pride, I would promptly take them back to my cell and proceed to mark them up with a red pen. And I'd always take special care to write little notes in the margins to tell him how ridiculous he was, how he was dumbing himself down, and how he wrote too many run-on sentences. Sam ignored everything I said completely. Because, to him, writing has never been about syntax or sentence structure or grammatical detail. No, to Sam, good writing revolves around one thing and only one thing facts.

"Sam," I would say, "why do you insist on writing about these things - things like credit and finance, and law? Is that really the stuff you're passionate about?"

"Yeah, it is," he would say simply. "These things are the foundations of becoming a financial success. These are functional, real-world things. They're the nuts and bolts of gaining and maintaining wealth." I would nod as if in agreement. And, really, it's not like I didn't agree with him. I did. I understood the importance of practical concerns, the importance of understanding the finer points of economic maneuvering, and the nuanced verbiage of legal documents. Sure, those things had their place. Yet, frankly, they weren't exactly the kind of things that got my blood pumping. But Sam? Sam was a different story. Almost daily, I would listen to him excitedly talk about some obscure law he'd uncovered or some little-known financial loophole that incarcerated people stood to benefit from. Occasionally, to himself, he'd say, "Man... if only people knew."

It went on like this for weeks, but then one day something seemed to click in Sam. He came marching down to the dayroom and slammed a big stack of files on the table where I was sitting. Alarmed, I looked up. "What the hell's all that?" "Research," he sighed.

"Research... for what?" Sam stood up straight and declared, "I'm gonna write it.

I scrunched up my face and asked, "You're gonna write what?"

"The book that every inmate in this country doesn't even know they need yet."

"That's bold and ambitious. How do you plan on doing that?"

I wish I hadn't asked - because for the next three hours, I was fated to become Sam's one-man captive audience. I'd never before seen a man so passionate about writing a financial education book for inmates. He spoke like a man possessed, like a guy who'd finally found something noble to pursue after years of disinterest. As he spoke, leaping confidently from one subject to another, it slowly began to dawn on me that Sam genuinely knew what he was talking about. The thoughts were tumbling out of him so breathlessly that several times I had to ask him to slow down, if not for his sake, for mine, because I was genuinely struggling with all the threads he was weaving together at once.

By the end of that dayroom, my mind was reeling. And, to tell you the truth, the next day I half expected Sam to have forgotten all about it. Surely, I thought, he'd just been in a manic stage-he didn't really plan on writing that book, did he? But, that evening, when I looked through my cell door, there he was sitting at that same table with that huge stack of files next to him, his pen quickly moving back and forth across the page. And, sure enough, he was out there every night thereafter, writing a book to give every inmate a real, cut-and-dried financial education - the book that every inmate in the country didn't know they needed yet.

And that's what the Jailhouse Financial Playbook is. It's about providing inmates with the crucial information and resources they need to start making the kind of intelligent, informed financial decisions that can change the trajectory of the rest of their lives. This book is a clear, easy-to-read guide that simplified many of the complicated financial methods and loopholes available to incarcerated people. Put simply, this is a book designed to give prisoners the tools and knowledge they need to take back control of their financial future.

In parting, there's one more thing I want to say. Prison is hard. If you're incarcerated, you already know this. You know what it is to be separated from loved ones, to feel like you have no purpose, and to live in the shadow of a shameful past. As a prisoner, you know what it is to have a profoundly uncertain future. And, as a man who's been in prison for over a decade, I understand.

But so does Sam. He's been in our shoes. He's faced the same demons, and, against overwhelming odds, he's learned how to succeed. So follow the steps he's laid out. Use the resources he's provided. And more than anything else, trust in your own potential. Believe in yourself.

Because it is amazing what can be achieved from a prison dayroom.

INTRODUCTION

DEAR READER,

First off, I'd like to start by thanking you for buying my book and for supporting not only me, but everyone on the team that's involved in my newly found legitimate hustle. It means the world to all of us who work so hard to make all this possible, most of us, including myself, from our prison cells. Without you, there would be none of this. It's because of you all of this is even possible.

I sincerely hope that this book helps you just as it has for me and so many other inmates across the country. As you can imagine, because I'm publishing this from prison, usually everything I try to do is incredibly difficult and challenging, and that especially includes promoting and trying to get the word out to people on the outside and in other state prisons about my books. That's why it would mean everything to me, and everyone involved if you could help out by reviewing the books, posting about them on your social media, and spreading the word to family, friends, co-workers, and anyone you know that's incarcerated. Let them know Sam Ferraro and his company, The Prisoner Press, aren't playing around with this publishing game. All of my books are a must-read for everybody, especially those who are incarcerated and out on parole, as well as their families and friends.

These aren't just your average prisoner self-help type of books and I'm definitely not your average author, so therefore, to understand my credibility, my perspective, experience, and knowledge, you first must understand a little about me and the fucked-up life that I've lived. This life taught me everything that I know and now share with you. Because of that fucked-up life I chose to live, I have spent most of my twenties and now the beginning of my thirties locked up, whether it was in county jail, state prison, or a court-ordered inpatient drug treatment rehab.

Most people, if they were in my situation, (32 years old, having already wasted their twenties behind bars and now back in prison again), would have given up, even before catching the new case and being sentenced to prison for a fourth time. I see it literally every day in prison. They give up on life, and more often sooner than later, they break down and accept the fact that they believe they're destined to an inevitable state of living between two equally, and just as terrible life sentences: one as a criminal and drug addict living that lifestyle out on the street, and the other as an inmate locked up in prison. This is a spiral I had come way too close to falling into myself. Without any doubt, I would have if it hadn't been for the success I've had with this company, my books, and everything that I've been able to accomplish, against all odds, while in prison for my fourth and absolutely last time ever. You can bet on that. This is no longer the life I'm down with having, now that I've proven to myself I can be so much more.

Then, there are those like me who aren't necessarily stronger or better than anyone, just different in every sense of the word. We're the type who are just too damn stubborn to ever just give up like that and let the universe win. Although, as beneficial as having such a strong, relentless personality can be, it can just as easily be the cause of your downfall, just as it has ultimately been mine. It has caused so much destruction all throughout my life and is the reason that I have spent so many years in prison. After I complete my current six-year sentence, I will have a total of 14 years in prison altogether. Bruh, that's fucking crazy just thinking about it!

Through all the setbacks, hard times, and losses I've taken, as well as my best years wasted in prison, do you think that I've ever given up or lost my drive and ambition to become wealthy and successful? FUCK, NO! Not even a little bit. I've just had to learn to approach matters in different ways since I'm limited to what I can do while I'm incarcerated. But that never stopped me. You're reading the proof right now of just how different I really am. Who goes to prison, finds success, and turns their sentence into a legitimate business venture and themselves into a jailhouse entrepreneur? Me, that's who! And I'm only just getting started chasing this legal paper.

And that's not even the craziest part. I'm going to let you in on something that you probably won't believe. It's that you can just as easily get to my level and become as rich and successful as I am. And I'm going to help you do it. Throughout my book, I give you the game and all of the cheat codes that you'll need to build the foundation to become successful both while you're still incarcerated and when you get back out onto the streets.

The only thing that can stop you from being successful is you. We are always going to be our very own worst enemy and find excuses for everything. Believe me, I know all about that. Only now I've eliminated all the excuses you could come up with as to why you can't do what I've done and become successful. So now you can use all your energy on actually doing it rather than trying to find reasons why you can't, because let's be real: If I, of all people, can do it, and do it all while in prison, then you definitely can.

You can't do it because you're locked up...

Bruh, smh. That's like the easiest excuse ever that you can use for just about everything, and also it's absolutely an untrue and bullshit excuse! After reading this, you won't ever be able to legitimately use that excuse again. That's because you'll know that whatever it is that you want to accomplish, you'll be able to do it if you really want to. Being locked up isn't some permanent roadblock preventing you from doing what you want, It's just another obstacle in your path to money and success that you'll have to figure out how to get around. I had to, when it came time to figure out how to overcome all the restrictions and limitations of being incarcerated, to be able to publish a book and start my own company. After hard work and dedication, I overcame all the challenges and prevailed. Everything I've done thus far; I've done legitimately, and every dollar I've made has been from inside prison.

So, if that's what is stopping you, then you discovered the right series to read, because everything in my books and legal guides are predominantly for prisoners and ex-offenders.

You can't because you know nothing about legitimate hustles or business...

My first time in prison, I was just 20 years old, and I didn't know shit about anything except for, of course, fucking my life up and getting into trouble. I was already an expert on that well before my twenties. I knew nothing about business or that there was even such a thing as hustling legally. Then, on my second bid, when I was twenty-three, I started learning about business. But as much as I taught myself about business and all the many ways to hustle legally, I stupidly assumed and for so long that it wasn't even possible for an inmate to start their own business, publish books, or do really any legit business out in the world while in prison. That was until a couple years ago in the beginning of this bid, I picked up the right book and learned how wrong I was all of these years, that It is actually very possible for us inmates to do, and that's what sparked my dedication to learn how to hustle legally from prison.

You think you don't have the ability to be successful in prison; you're not like me...

That's exactly the self-defeating mindset that'll stop you from ever accomplishing anything worthwhile in your life, just as it did for so many years with me. And it's that kind of negative bullshit thinking you're going to have to change, and do it quickly, if you're ever going to have a chance at becoming wealthy and successful. Stop trying to compare yourself with others. That never ends well, and it will only end up driving you crazy. Trust me here, it has absolutely nothing to do with whether or not you're like me, because, straight up, there's nothing that I have done to make money, become successful, and win at life legally that you can't do yourself, as long as you follow my game plan and put the work in.

You can't because you're broke and think you don't have enough money to do anything legitimate...

Bruh, you really think you're the only one in that situation, because you're not. No one who is in prison or who has just come home on parole has any real money, and they sure as hell don't have enough money to even think about starting a business or doing anything like that.

The truth is that most normal working-class people out there don't have the money either. Here's some advice you should hold on to. Money makes everything easier, but it's not actually necessary to have, because it's been my experience over and over again that as long as you want something bad enough, you'll find a way to get it. A perfect example of that is me.

I published my first book and started my own company right in the beginning of this bid when I was tapped out between paying my attorney, who was really worthless because he didn't actually do anything that a public defender couldn't do for me for free and wasting the rest of my money in the county jail on drugs and commissary. I was broke as hell, surviving in prison off of my little $30 per month work pay. I knew that I couldn't go through my entire bid being broke like that, and so I started figuring out different creative ways to hustle and stack up enough money to afford to self-publish my first book. So yeah, you really can't get much lower than where I started from.

In fact, if it hadn't been for that struggle when I first arrived at prison, I never would've had the money-hungry desperation that had pushed me to think outside the box to come up with new ways to earn money from other inmates in prison. That determination was what got me up off the bunk, out of my self-defeating feelings, and was how I started creating my game plan to map out exactly how I would become wealthy and successful, not just while I was in prison, but for the rest of my life, the very same one that I'm now putting you on to so you can have the same if not even more success in your life, whether it's in prison or out on the streets!

Without that determination and my money-motivated drive, I never would've picked up a pen to create that game plan, written my first book, or ever come up with the idea to publish it through my own company. And, of course without them, I never would've accomplished any of the many other things that I have been able to do over the past years and be where I am today, which is still in prison, but unlike how I had come in. At least now I'm on an entirely different level of the game. I have money, success, and I even have a couple more titles to put after my name rather than just Inmate QP4526: CEO, Business and Self-Help Guru, and my favorite, newest title, Published Author.

I owe everything to the struggle that I have endured, because as hard as the journey has been, it not only has made me the successful businessman and legit paper-chasing entrepreneur that I am today, but it has taught me so much about so many different things: money, business, life, people, and most importantly about myself and what all I'm really capable of accomplishing, even while at my lowest.

The Prisoner Press and the multimedia platform that I have created for all of you is an extension of myself. Just like how I was doing it back when I was out on the streets, putting everyone I knew on to get money with me, I'm still doing it even now while I'm down. The only difference now is that instead of high-risk, illegal money, I'm putting everyone on to my new life and game plan to chase after real, sustainable success and get to this legitimate paper with me.

I may not have started applying all of what I've learned until these last couple years, but over the many years that I have spent being locked up, I have taught myself just about everything that there is to know about business, how to hustle and win legally, so much so that it has become my new favorite addiction and the only healthy one I've ever had that actually puts money into my pockets, not just empties them out.

The most common path for people who want to get into business is to go to a university and attend classes to learn about it a few times a week for four years. I've been reading and studying every day for almost ten years now. So yeah, although I might not have a fancy college degree to hang on the wall to show off, trust and believe that I know more than most who do. As much as I know about business, and that's quite a bit, I know even more about the criminal justice system and living the fast lifestyle as a criminal.

Over the years, I have learned many, many different ways anyone, regardless of their background, can make all kinds of real money by hustling legally, whether you're in prison or out on the streets. But the one the thing that I've learned and probably the most important, is that being a criminal just ain't the wave anymore. More than that, crime and the whole fast lifestyle is played out.

This isn't me selling out or switching up all of a sudden because I've gone legit. That's never the type of time I'll ever be on at all. I'm not saying this to appeal to what society deems socially acceptable or to be politically correct. That is not my argument here, nor is it ever my intention.

No, I'm saying this to be real with you and try to hopefully get through to you to save your life. Even though if you're anything like the old me, then you're most likely too stubborn to listen to anything that I have to say, and unfortunately must learn everything the hardest possible way there is every time. Even though the answer may be right in front of you, so easily accessible, you go out of your way to do it the hard way.

I will be the first to admit that back not so long ago, when I was out living that life, no one could have convinced me to ever stop living the way that I was and walk away from any of it. It took me having to come back to prison for a fourth time to finally get me to let it all go and to actually want something better for myself. I finally was through risking my life out there, running the streets and living the fast life just to end up always losing everything that I worked so hard to get and coming in and out of prison. Admittedly, I was addicted to that entire crazy-ass, high-octane, fast money, drug-fueled, can't-tell-me-shit lifestyle. I really lived like I was the Prince of Philly.

When I was out there, I wanted it more than anything else, including getting high. As with any real addiction, living the fast criminal lifestyle, there was never any middle ground. Either you were all the way up living what definitely felt like your absolute best life or you weren't, and you were drowning at your rock bottom. But the fucked-up thing about addiction is, as horrible as the lows always are, it's those times that you are up feeling the full effects of the high that hooks you and makes you chase after it no matter what. And once you're addicted, whether it's drugs, sex, or living the fast lifestyle like it was for me, the highs are so euphoric that it's worth enduring the lows and doing whatever you have to just to get back up to that level of feeling like you're the king of the world, or in my case, the Prince of Philly.

When I was up, I had more money than I did sense, and because of that, my dumb ass wasted every dollar that I made on all the wrong shit: fake friends, expensive cars, condos, jewelry, designer clothes and shoes, women, whether they were college girls, hookers, or porn stars, drugs, partying, trips, and any other stupid thing I could think of wasting all my money on without ever once saving or investing any of it. I was

18

young, dumb, and thought that was what life was all about. If only I had the sense to save and invest even a portion of the money I was making back then, I would've been a millionaire years ago. There's no telling where I'd be right now - not in a prison cell, that's for certain.

As an addict, we are only just one bad decision away from relapsing and fucking our lives right back up no matter how far we may have come. Scary thought, but it's the reality that we live every day. And if I'm keeping it all the way one hundred percent honest, even with all my success and the legitimate money that I'm making now, I would give it all up without any hesitation and go right back to getting high and living my old lifestyle as the Prince of Philly if there was even the slightest possibility that I could get away with doing it without ending up right back in prison or dead.

But, the way things are now on the streets, no matter what you may want to believe, those are the only two outcomes. The good old days when you could actually have a real shot at having a successful long run in this life, where you hustle doing what you do, stack your paper, invest it into something legitimate, and then get out of the game clean, are dead and gone.

Straight up, that shit is over. Nowadays, you're either going to be caught by the cops and sent to prison, and that's If you're lucky, because if not, you're going to end up getting taken out by your ops and put on a t-shirt.

These young boys have turned the streets into a war zone where you can't even hustle and make money out there anymore. They're shooting people right out in public with no regard in broad daylight every day over nothing. It's just like a video game to them and not real life. So that's why I say crime is played all the way out. It's not strategically intelligent to do anymore, especially under today's circumstances. Not only are all the risks you have to take just to commit a crime huge, and the losses you'll take will almost always outweigh what you gain, but because with all the legitimate opportunities out there available to everyone with today's technology and resources, it's not even necessary to take the risk.

For all those reasons and more, I'm through with the whole lifestyle and being a career criminal and drug addict. I refuse to once again be another statistic for recidivism ever again. It has become my passion to learn how to make more money legally than I ever did illegally, so that when I'm finally released from prison, I can ball just as hard as I did, only this time I'll do it much smarter and without the risk of doing anything that would potentially send me back to prison or get me killed over. Not only has It become my passion to learn it and make money by hustling legally but also to share my knowledge and teach it to others just like me who want to make just as much money and live the same lavish balling lifestyle as they did before when they were living the criminal lifestyle but do it now legitimately without any of the danger and risks.

That's exactly what my series. The Shit Prisoners Need to Know - is all about. I've created it to provide inmates, ex-offenders, addicts, and anyone else who wants it with the game plan, knowledge, tools, and everything else you need to become successful, overcome addiction, beat parole at their own game, change your life, stay out of jail, and hustle legally and win at life!

So, are you ready? You ready to get it? You ready to change your life and become a Jailhouse Entrepreneur for real? Then let's get this legitimate paper together and start winning!

Sincerely, your friend,
Sam Ferraro

PARTONE

PRISONERPERSONALFINANCE, CREDIT,DEBTMANAGMENTCOURSE

Introduction

This series is dedicated to giving prisoners the real life knowledge and battle-tested game plans that they need to know, but no one ever tells them. In my books, I help break down everything that you need to know in order for you to achieve legitimate success and wealth through legal hustles in the most unlikely place in the world- prison.

Everything that I put you on to and all the knowledge that I give you throughout the series is the exact same game plan that I have used to teach myself how to overcome challenges, be proactive, get my mind right, hustle legally, achieve success, and ultimately change my life forever by becoming a Jailhouse Entrepreneur. I have stamped the books in my series 100% Prisoner-Certified and have all been proven to really work by me, and by all of the prisoners and ex-offenders across the country who have become rich and successful both in and out of prison because they picked up my book, applied the knowledge, and followed my game plans.

This first part of the book teaches you everything that you need to know to improve your credit score, learn how to use loopholes in the law to remove accurate debt from off your credit file, move your money from your inmate account to an outside bank account so the prison doesn't have control over all your money, and how to choose the right person to designate as your Power of Attorney in order for you to become financially independent from the Department of Corrections so you are able to conduct your business as you see fit.

LESSON 1

Why You Should Give a Shit About Your Credit

If you're like I was just a few years ago, or any of the thousands of inmates doing time in prison, you probably don't give a shit about how much debt you owe or whether or not you currently have good credit, because let's face it: things like that don't really mater while you're in prison. In your mind, those are street problems that you'll deal with once you get back out on the street. They're not prison problems you need to worry about right now. Well, though you might like to believe that, I've learned that is the wrong type of mindset to have if you want to ever become successful.

Being incarcerated puts a hold on many aspects of your life, but not everything. You want to know exactly how to become rich and successful while you're in prison? You do it by always thinking proactively. It's as simple as waking up every morning and asking yourself the million dollar question: What can I do with all this unused free time I have? How can I improve myself and my life spiritually, emotionally, physically, and financially? These are questions you should be asking yourself every day for the rest of your life, not just while you're in prison.

I have learned that becoming successful is as much about mindset as it is about what you actually do. That's why it's taken me so long to get to where I am now, at least financially, because I'm still in prison. I had the desire, means, ideas, and the drive - everything I thought I needed - but my mind wasn't right. I have ADHD, ADD, Bipolar (all the good stuff), so for me, it was even more of a challenge to get my mind to a place where it worked in sync with my goals instead of against them.

It's all about being consistent and having a set routine to follow. For me, if I wake up and don't follow my morning routine, then I feel off for the rest of the day. I wake up for count at 6:00 a.m., plug the stinger in to heat water for my coffee, knock out my sets of pushups, watch News Nation while I eat breakfast (ever since COVID, they bring all the meals to our cells), shave, brush my teeth, wash my face, etc. Then, before the jail opens at 8:15 a.m., I sit at the desk and plan out what I'm going to do for that day.

Even if you're not like me and you don't need the structure of a daily routine as much as I do, having consistency and structure in your life is a key factor if you want to become successful. Of course, how you answer that question will almost always change daily. It doesn't matter how you answer or what it is you do as long as you come up with at least something that will move you closer to improving yourself and becoming successful. You may not want to follow an elaborate routine like mine, and that's fine. Your routine can literally just be waking up, asking yourself the million-dollar question every day, and coming up with an answer, no matter how big or small it may be for that day, and doing it.

The most important thing for you is to always keep in the back of your mind is that the possibilities of what you can achieve are limitless, even while you're in prison. It's all about taking the right steps towards becoming successful. And that starts right now with this book. I will give you the game plan to develop the foundation that you'll need to build your success, this however, is just the first stage to becoming successful, there are many. In the fourth book of this series, I'll teach you everything you need to know about the second stage, which is discovering what it is that you actually want to do to become rich and successful.

If you're looking for a good way to answer that million-dollar question in the morning, I'll help you out. A really effective way for you to improve your life and set yourself up to be in an excellent financial position once you're back out on the streets is for you to start working towards repairing your credit now. Why wait until you get out to get started when you have all the time in the world right now to begin the lengthy process of repairing bad credit?

Trust me, you want to start it now so when you get out, not only will you walk out of prison ahead of the game by having excellent credit, but it will be one less thing you'll have to deal with as you start to put your life back together.

So Why Should You Give a Shit About Your Credit?

Having lived a predominantly cash lifestyle myself, as most prisoners have, I know it's easy to forget how important it is to have good credit. But if you plan on living a legitimate life once you get out of prison, then you better start making it a priority to start rebuilding your credit now. Because unless you're coming home to a bunch of money- let's be real - most of you aren't, you will require good credit for just about everything.

And rebuilding your credit takes time. In most cases, if your credit score has dropped to below 500, it may take years. That's why right now, while you're incarcerated, is the best time for you to start the long process of improving your credit. Because not only do you have all the time in the world to do it, but you're also not using it. Of course, it may be hard to dedicate a lot of time and effort into fixing something you can't actually use, but trust me, if you don't take this opportunity to rebuild your credit, I promise you'll regret it as soon as you hit the streets.

Still not a good enough reason to make you give a shit?

Okay, think about it this way, then. Every one of us, while we're doing time, regardless of whether you're doing a year or down for life, dream about all the things you want to do, trips you want to take, and stuff you want to buy once you're released back to the streets.

For many of us, all we'd really have to do once we get out of prison is go right back to our old criminal life to start making fast money again. If we did that, all the dreams we had every night lying in our bunk might be brought to life in no time. Of course, by going back down that same path that led us to prison in the first place, we'd be taking a huge gamble on our lives. How things are nowadays, if you step back into life, there's no guarantee you'll make it long enough in the game to even earn enough money or have enough time to do anything with it, for real.

Now ask yourself this: If you're not trying to be about that life when you go home - if you don't want to gamble anymore with your freedom, then how are you going to afford to buy that new car you saw in Car and Driver? How can you pay to take your girl on a trip somewhere nice? Where are you going to find the money for that down payment on an apartment? Hell, how are you going to be able to afford anything at all when you just come home from prison and have no money?

Even if you're one of the few people who come out of prison financially set, you'll still need to have good credit for fundamental things like renting an apartment, getting cheaper car insurance, and even signing up for essential services like a cell phone, Internet, and utilities.

Now, if you're like the majority of people who come out of prison with little to no money at all, then you better take rebuilding your credit seriously, right now, while you're locked up. If you do, and you build up your credit score to a decent number (700 or above) by using the proven methods I'll put you on to, then once you're released and back out in the world, things will be so much easier for you.

Take it from someone who's done this three different times so far. The first two times, at ages 23 and 26, I came out of prison broke as fuck with the lowest credit scores possible. And, let me tell you, shit was so rough for me that both times I didn't even make it more than a couple months before I gave up trying. I stopped reporting to parole and jumped right back into the mix. But my last time out was a little different, at least in the beginning. In 2020, I left prison with a hefty Cash App full of money that I'd saved up from hustling during my bid and damn near an 800 credit score. I'd managed to get that credit score from using the same exact methods I give you in this book.

So when I tell you all of this is proven, you know I really did everything that I'm putting you on to. And it worked out just the way I said it did. Obviously, having money and good credit made the transition from prison back into society (and all that comes with it) so much easier. I was able to actually accomplish a lot, including starting my very first business. And if I had stayed on that path - and never let my addiction, self-destructive tendencies, and general impulsive stupidity get the best of me - I would have become a legitimate millionaire years ago. I definitely wouldn't be writing this right now from a prison cell.

When you're released from prison, you're going to need many things that you likely won't be able to afford. Everyone always thinks about all the big things they'll need, but what most people don't realize is the many little things they'll need as well. The little things will quickly add up to just as much - if not more - than some of the larger things. Please, just keep that in mind when you start planning for your release.

There are a lot of resources out there for ex-offenders. I mean, shit, look at how many books have been written on the subject of re-entry for ex-offenders. Hell, I'm even writing one to cash in on the trend. But my reason for writing a book like this is different from other authors. Other authors write about re-entry because they have psychology degrees, or maybe they worked in corrections their whole lives. Those are people who made careers out of dispensing life advice through cell doors to guys like you and me. I don't know about you, but the last thing I want to do is buy a book written by one of those assholes - people who love to act like they know what it's like but really have no fucking clue.

But this book is different. This is a book for prisoners by a prisoner. So when I tell you that you're going to need good credit when you go home, you better believe my words are coming from hard experience. Sure, there are government assistance programs and nonprofits that will help you here and there, but these programs aren't nearly as helpful as you think, and you're going to be mostly on your own out there.

Unless you have financial support from family and friends or you're going out to a job that's already set up, then you're going to be in a tough situation when you get out. Most people are when they come home from prison.

If it sounds like you should be more intimidated than excited to go back to the streets. That's because for real you should be! Doing time in prison is easy compared to having to survive out in the world. It sounds so fucked up, I know, but it's the truth.

Reintegrating back into the community is scary and full of uncertainty. There will be challenges, setbacks, and a hell of a lot of struggles. I wish I could give you the cheat code to make it fun and easy, but if such a thing exists, I haven't found it yet.

The closest thing to a cheat code I've found is having good credit. With good credit, many of your initial financial challenges can be easily solved. Coming out of prison, you're going to need the basic essentials: clothes, hygiene items, food, a cell phone, furniture, and electronics for your apartment, and sooner or later, a vehicle. The list goes on and on. Life out there is expensive. And, if you're anything like me, you're for sure going to want a few dollars to spend on having some fun your first night home.

Let's keep it all the way real. We all know that life. We know the game inside and out. Being out there hustling - that's our comfort zone. Committing crimes, getting money fast, and blowing it even faster, getting high- all that stuff is scary to normal people, but it was normal, everyday life for people like us. Yet, switching up, leaving that life to go legit and live a "normal" life out there - that shit scares the hell out of us. Having to find a real job, save money, stay sober, pay bills, struggle paycheck to paycheck to get on your feet - that is fucking terrifying for us. It certainly is for me.

But they say the best way to truly understand something is to teach it. So that's what I'm doing. Let's get started.

LESSON 2

Getting a Copy of Your Free Credit Report

In this lesson, you will learn, one, how to get a copy of your credit report, and two, I will break down everything you need to know to understand the report.

Everyone, even prisoners, is by law entitled to get a free report from each of the three major Credit Reporting Agencies (CRAs) - Experian, Equifax, and TransUnion - every year. Thanks to the Fair Credit Reporting Act, (FCRA), there are several additional ways to get a free credit report. You qualify for a free report if you:

- Are unemployed and intend to apply for a job within 60 days
- Are receiving public welfare assistance
- Think any of the CRA reports contain inaccurate information about you due to fraud
- Have been denied credit or insurance within the past 60 days

Requesting Your Credit Report

As an incarcerated person, you only have two options for getting copies of your report:

1. The first option is to have someone on the outside who you trust pull your credit reports from the Internet and mail them to you, of course. This requires you to give out all your most sensitive information to the person for them to access your credit file online. This is why it's important you choose only someone that you absolutely trust.

Otherwise, you take the risk of possibly falling victim to identity theft and having someone living it up out there all at your expense.

2. The second, and much safer option for you, is to just go through the prison to get copies of your credit report. Typically, I never advocate for you to use prison "inside" resources if you have an option to do it yourself with the help of your people. However, in this particular situation, I have found through my own experience that the prison actually is the better option in terms of safety and ease.

And, as many resources I have on the streets between my family, support network, business partners, attorney, accountant, and everyone else, I still go to my block counselor every year to obtain copies of my credit report.

The Process of Getting Your Credit Report Through the Prison

This is the process that I have to do to get copies of my credit reports. Sure, I'm in Pennsylvania, and it may be different in other state prisons, but generally it's all the same across the country. At the end of the day, prison is prison.

Write to your block counselor or unit manager and inform him/her that you would like to obtain a copy of your Free Annual Credit Report

- Once they process your request, the counselor will provide you with two forms for you to fill out:

    a) Annual Credit Report Request Form, and

    b) Release of information DOC form

- In order to have your Annual Credit Report Request

form processed, they require you to include proof of identification. This is where the Release of Information DOC form comes into play. By signing the form, you give the prison permission to send a copy of your DOC face card (This is as official as a state picture ID card.)

- That's all there is to it. Allow two to three weeks for your first CRA report to arrive. Typically, by the end of a month, you'll have all three credit reports.

How to Interpret Your Credit Report

Once you receive your Free Credit Report, you might feel a little overwhelmed by the volume of information. That's okay. Just take a deep breath and slowly review each listing. Hopefully, you won't find anything you don't recognize. If you do, we'll discuss in a later chapter the steps you'll need to take to dispute questionable listings. But, for the time being, let's focus on what credit reports are comprised of.

On your credit report, you'll find the following information:

- Bankruptcies
- Foreclosures
- Liens

If you lose a lawsuit, a person can place a lien against your real estate. When this happens, you cannot sell the property until you've paid off the lien.

- Loans, whether you've paid them back or not
- Each credit card you've owned over the last seven years
- Credit applications you've made
- Credit applications approved

34

- Credit applications rejected
- Payments you've made on time

Payments you haven't made on time. For each account on your credit report, these details are cited:

- The account's opening and closing dates
- The amount owed
- The interest rate
- The monthly payment amount
- The day of your last payment
- The high balance and the balance yet unpaid
- Your payment history for that listing

It's important for you to know that bankruptcies and liens will stay on your credit report for up to ten years, while all other listings only stay on for seven years.

Banks and other financial institutions use your credit report to decide whether or not you are creditworthy. If you have a record of making late payments, it's going to be much more difficult for you to get credit. If you do get credit, your interest rate will likely be a lot higher, so always try to make timely payments.

The Importance of Your FICO Score

Your credit report isn't the only thing creditors look at. Potential lenders will also review your FICO credit score. FICO scores are the three-digit credit ratings derived from your credit history. They're calculated by Fair, Isaac & Company, a financial company in California. And, if you want to improve your credit, you're going to want to pay close attention to your FICO score.

FICO credit ratings range from 300 at the lowest to 850 at the highest. You want to shoot for, at least, around a 750. According to Fair, Isaac & Company, here's how your FICO scores are determined:

- **Your Payment History (35%):** This is the single most important factor in your credit score. Bankruptcies, collections, and even one late payment can hurt your score. And keep in mind that current problems count more than older ones.

- **Amount of Debt (30%):** Total amount owed, the number of your accounts with outstanding balances, and how much of your credit you're actually utilizing, matter here. The more you owe, the lower your FICO score will be. That's why, interestingly enough, declaring bankruptcy can sometimes boost your credit score (because it gets rid of your debt.)

- **Credit History Length (15%):** This factors in how long you've had accounts open - your oldest, your newest, and the collective average. You want to have accounts open that you've been using for a long time, but if you don't use an account any longer, you want to close it.

- **Amount of New Credit (10%):** Every loan application shows up on your credit score as a "hard inquiry." Too many of them in too short a window of time can hurt your score.

- **Your Credit Mix (10%):** You want to have a variety of debt spread across loans, credit cards, mortgages, etc. A healthy variety shows potential creditors you can manage all types of credit.

Even though FICO scores are important, they may not show up on every credit report. So, besides requesting a credit report, it would also be smart to request your FICO score specifically. To make things a bit easier, I've included a copy of an "Annual Credit Report Request Form" from annualcreditreport.com. If you're able, go to the prison library, print off a copy, fill it out, give it to your counselor, and have them mail it to the address below to get your free credit report.

Annual Credit Report Request Service

P.O. Box 105281

Atlanta, GA 30348-5201

EQUIFAX :experian. TransUnion

Annual Credit Report Request Form

You have the right to get a free copy of your credit file disclosure, commonly called a credit report, once every 12 months, from each of the nationwide consumer credit reporting companies, Equifax, Experian and TransUnion.
For instant access to your free credit report, visit www.annualcreditreport.com.

For more information on obtaining your free credit report, visit www.annualcreditreport.com or call 877-322-8228.

Use this form if you prefer to write to request your credit report from any, or all, of the nationwide consumer credit reporting companies. The following information is required to process your request. Omission of any information may delay your request.

Once complete, fold (do not staple or tape), place into a #10 envelope, affix required postage and mail to:
Annual Credit Report Request Service P.O. Box 105281 Atlanta, GA 30348-5281.

Please use a Black or Blue Pen and write your responses in PRINTED CAPITAL LETTERS without touching the sides of the boxes like the examples listed below:

A B C D E F G H I J K L M N O P Q R S T U V W X Y Z   0 1 2 3 4 5 6 7 8 9

Social Security Number:

☐☐☐ - ☐☐ - ☐☐☐☐

Date of Birth:

☐☐ / ☐☐ / ☐☐☐☐
Month   Day   Year

— Fold Here —   — Fold Here —

First Name   M.I.

Last Name   JR, SR, III, etc.

Current Mailing Address:

House Number   Street Name

Apartment Number / Private Mailbox   For Puerto Rico Only: Print Urbanization Name

City   State   ZipCode

Previous Mailing Address (complete only if at current mailing address for less than two years):

House Number   Street Name

— Fold Here —   — Fold Here —

Apartment Number / Private Mailbox   For Puerto Rico Only: Print Urbanization Name

City   State   ZipCode

Shade Circle Like This → ●

Not Like This → ☒ ☒

I want a credit report from (shade each that you would like to receive):
○ Equifax
○ Experian
○ TransUnion

○ Shade here if, for security reasons, you want your credit report to include no more than the last four digits of your Social Security Number.

If additional information is needed to process your request, the consumer credit reporting company will contact you by mail.

Your request will be processed within 15 days of receipt and then mailed to you.

Copyright 2025, Central Source LLC

31238

Sample Credit Report Denial Letter

Dear SAM FERRARO:

We received your request for a copy of Your Equifax Credit report. However, we need additional information in order to verify your identity and address. To help us fulfill your request, please send us a letter with your full name, Social Security Number, current address, and your date of birth. Please also include a copy of a document verifying your identity (ex: driver's license or birth certificate), your Social Security Number (ex: Social Security card or W2 form), and a copy of a document verifying your address (ex: utility bill or pay stub).

Please return all required information and a copy of this letter to:

Equifax Information Services, LLC

P.O. Box 740241

Atlanta, GA 30374-0241

We were unable to locate a credit file in our database with the identification information you provided. In order to further assist you, we will need additional documents to verify your identification. Please provide your complete name, current, and former addresses, Social Security Number, and date of birth. We ask that you please send us a copy of two different items - one from each of the two categories listed below. One item will verify your identity, and the other will verify your current address.

Category 1) IDENTIFICATION

Please make a copy of one of the following Items:

The item you choose must contain your 9-digit Social Security number.

- Pay stub with complete U.S. Social Security number
- W-2 form with complete U.S. Social Security number
- Valid Social Security card
- Driver's License

Note: A 'Work Permit Only' card is not valid proof of an SSN

Category 2) CURRENT ADDRESS

Please make a copy of one of the following Items:

The item you choose MUST contain your current mailing address of PO BOX 33028, St. Petersburg, FL, 33733-8028

- Rental/lease agreement or house deed
- Pay stub with address
- Utility bill (i.e., gas, electric, water, cable, residential telephone bill) with current service address.

Again, we need a total of two items-one from each of the categories above-to process your request. Please submit those Items along with this letter to the following address:

Equifax Information Services, LLC

P.O. Box 105069

Atlanta, GA 30348-5069

*Simply filling out a copy of the Annual Credit Report Request Form and mailing it in will not work. I tried it the first time myself, and the above letter was sent back to me.

That's why you have to get with your counselor. They'll be able to help you out with the necessary documents.

POWER OF ATTORNEY

As much as a motivated individual is able to do and accomplish from prison, there is just as much they can't do without help from someone on the outside. That's just the reality faced by all inmate entrepreneurs. So if you don't already have someone on the outside who is helping you, then you better start looking for someone, because later in the lesson, you will complete an exercise created to help you choose the right person to designate as your Power of Attorney, also known as your "Agent."

As you should know, being financially independent and in control of your money, especially while you're incarcerated, is extremely important. Likewise, it is equally important that you have someone in your corner who is trustworthy and reliable to help you manage your finances from prison. This person can be anyone out on the streets - a family member, significant other, close friend, attorney, or even a company that offers reputable personal assistant services to inmates.

Understanding that you can't do certain things, this person will play a crucial part in your path to success because they will be your legs on the ground out there. They'll help you take control over all the different things that, as an incarcerated person, you have no control over. This will be the person you can depend on to set up your bank account if you can't open one yourself, to apply for credit cards, loans, file taxes, conduct business on your behalf, make purchases, and even pay bills at your request.

Being incarcerated, as many reading this know all too well, comes with a tremendous amount of challenges and setbacks, but as easy as it would be to use this as a cop-out, there's no excuse for you to not try. With a little drive and ambition, along with the right lessons and game plan, there is nothing that you can't overcome and achieve. But don't get it twisted. No one ever said becoming a Jailhouse Entrepreneur would be easy, but it is possible. By applying everything that I teach you in these lessons, you'll be well on your way to controlling your money, life, and having a very successful future.

In the following pages, I'll talk more about Power of Attorney and how to choose the right person to designate as your Agent. I include examples of Power of Attorney forms from my state, Pennsylvania. These forms may be different for your state, but they should give you an idea of what to expect. Read them closely so you understand exactly what powers you'll be giving up and handing over to the person you end up choosing.

Also, I have created an exercise to help you narrow down your list of candidates and choose the best possible person to become your designated Agent. It's through the same process that worked for me when coming up with my own Power of Attorney Agent, and one that I think will help you, too.

FINDING YOUR POWER OF ATTORNEY

EXERCISE

Finding the right person to be your Agent will be one of the most important decisions you will make while you're incarcerated. Who you ultimately designate could very easily make or break you. That's the reality of the power you are giving them over you, and why you must be absolutely certain that you're choosing the right person. Therefore I made this exercise to help walk you through the process of choosing the best possible person to be your Agent.

A. The first step is to come up with a list of five people. They can be anyone whom you trust the most in the world.

   1._____

   2._____

   3._____

   4._____

B. Now we're going to shorten the list down to three by doing some not so easy process of elimination. Just because you trust all five people that you listed above, and they all have your best interests at heart, it doesn't necessarily mean that they all are the right person for you to choose. Remember, whoever you end up choosing will have complete control over your money, assets, and basically your entire life while you're incarcerated or for however long you decide to keep them as your Agent.

Now think of one of the five people you listed who may not be the most responsible when it comes to managing their own personal finances, or who may not be very

organized - Probably not the ideal characteristics you want in someone who is in control of your money. Be honest with yourself. You may feel like you are obligated to choose a certain person by default because of who they are to you, whether it's your mom, girlfriend, baby mom, wife, or best friend, but that doesn't mean that you should. This is not personal. Your money and entire life is at stake. With that being said, list the three people you now think may be the right people for you.

1._____

2._____

3._____

C. It's not enough for the right person to be well organized and financially responsible. As important as those things are, it is even more important for them to be actually responsible. Yes, there is a difference. When making your decision consider the following: if someone doesn't consistently pick up when you call, responds back to your letters or emails in a timely manner, tends to forget or procrastinates to do things for you, or if they generally cannot be relied upon for assistance, then they're definitely not the right person to trust with managing your life.

That may or may not have helped narrow your list down. But this certainly will. You should choose someone who is, for the most part, neutral and who you know for sure, no matter what happens, will always, or at least for the entire duration of your incarceration, be in your life and have your back. Using that logic, that likely excludes; girlfriends, baby moms, friends, most relatives, and even some immediate family from being the kind of people that you want to have absolute power over your entire life. That's because they all have the potential to either ghost you for any reason at any time or, worse yet, use the power that you gave them against you if ever they become angry with you. Now you understand why this decision is so important for you to get right.

Here is some knowledge you will use for the rest of your life and be better for it. It has taken me having to go through a lot of shit to learn this about people. When you break it down to a fundamental level, there are only three true motives behind why a person continues to stay loyal to another person, especially when the person is incarcerated (out of sight, out of mind). They either love you, respect you, or are some way benefiting from you (usually financially). Understanding a person's true motive is a very powerful tool for you to have.

It's likely by now you have already made up your mind as to which of the original five you will choose to be your Agent out on the streets. However, if you haven't, then pick the two people that you believe will be the better choices out of the remaining three.

    1. _____

    2. _____

D. Now that you're down to the best two people, this is where it gets challenging. Because it could be that they are both equally as good to be the right person to be your Agent, making your decision that much harder. I have given you all of the characteristics you should look for in the one that you designate as your Agent, but I will leave you with one more factor to consider. I'm just going to assume, especially if you're reading this book, that you plan to convert your free time in prison into a money making hustle and start your own business. Then if that's the case, you may want to consider which of the two is more business savvy and has the most business experience. Now that you have all the knowledge to make the right choice. Who will it be?

POWER OF ATTORNEY

NOTICE

THE PURPOSE OF THIS POWER OF ATTORNEY IS TO GIVE THE PERSON YOU DESIGNATE (YOUR "AGENT) BROAD POWERS TO HANDLE YOUR PROPERTY, WHICH MAY INCLUDE POWERS TO SELL OR OTHERWISE DISPOSE OF ANY REAL OR PERSONAL PROPERTY WITHOUT ADVANCE NOTICE TO YOU OR APPROVAL BY YOU.

THIS POWER OF ATTORNEY DOES NOT IMPOSE A DUTY ON YOUR AGENT TO EXERCISE GRANTED POWERS, BUT, WHEN POWERS ARE EXERCISED, YOUR AGENT MUST USE DUE CARE TO ACT FOR YOUR BENEFIT AND IN ACCORDANCE WITH THIS POWER OF ATTORNEY.

YOUR AGENT MAY EXERCISE THE POWERS GIVEN HERE THROUGHOUT YOUR LIFETIME, EVEN AFTER YOU BECOME INCAPACITATED, UNLESS YOU EXPRESSLY LIMIT THE DURATION OF THESE POWERS OR YOU REVOKE THESE POWERS OR A COURT ACTING ON YOUR BEHALF TERMINATES YOUR AGENT'S AUTHORITY.

YOUR AGENT MUST ACT IN ACCORDANCE WITH YOUR REASONABLE EXPECTATIONS TO THE EXTENT ACTUALLY KNOWN BY YOUR AGENT AND, OTHERWISE, IN YOUR BEST INTEREST, ACT IN GOOD FAITH AND ACT ONLY WITHIN THE SCOPE OF AUTHORITY GRANTED BY YOU IN THE POWER OF ATTORNEY.

THE LAW PERMITS YOU, IF YOU CHOOSE, TO GRANT BROAD AUTHORITY TO AN AGENT UNDER POWER OF ATTORNEY, INCLUDING THE ABILITY TO GIVE AWAY ALL OF

YOUR PROPERTY WHILE YOU ARE ALIVE OR TO SUBSTANTIALLY CHANGE HOW YOUR PROPERTY IS DISTRIBUTED AT YOUR DEATH. BEFORE SIGNING THIS DOCUMENT, YOU SHOULD SEEK THE ADVICE OF AN ATTORNEY AT LAW TO MAKE SURE YOU UNDERSTAND IT.

A COURT CAN TAKE AWAY THE POWERS OF YOUR AGENT IF IT FINDS YOUR AGENT IS NOT ACTING PROPERLY.

THE POWERS AND DUTIES OF AN AGENT UNDER A POWER OF ATTORNEY ARE EXPLAINED MORE FULLY IN 20 P.A.C.S., CH. 56.

IF THERE IS ANYTHING ABOUT THIS FORM THAT YOU DO NOT UNDERSTAND, YOU SHOULD ASK A LAWYER OF YOUR OWN CHOOSING TO EXPLAIN IT TO YOU.

I HAVE READ OR HAD EXPLAINED TO ME THIS NOTICE, AND I UNDERSTAND ITS CONTENTS.

_____   _____

(PRINCIPAL)   (DATE) (DAY-MONTH-YEAR)

DURABLE POWER OF ATTORNEY ACKNOWLEDGEMENT AND ACCEPTANCE BY AGENT

I, _____, have read the attached Power of Attorney and am the person identified as the agent for the principal. I hereby acknowledge that when I act as agent: I shall act in accordance with the principal's reasonable expectations to the extent actually known by me and, otherwise, in the principal's best interest, act in good faith and act only within the scope of authority granted to me by the principal in the Power of Attorney.

_____

Signature of Agent

NAME:_____

UNIFORM STATUTORY FORM/POWER OF ATTORNEY

(Pennsylvania Consolidated Statutes Annotated) (Title 20 Pa. C.S.A. §5601)

NOTICE

THE POWERS GRANTED BY THIS DOCUMENT ARE BROAD AND SWEEPING. THEY ARE EXPLAINED IN CHAPTER 56 OF PENNSYLVANIA STATUTES AND CONSOLIDATION STATUTES ANNOTATED, TITLE 20 (5601-5604). THIS DOCUMENT DOES NOT AUTHORIZE ANYONE TO MAKE MEDICAL OR OTHER HEALTHCARE DECISIONS FOR YOU. YOU MAY REVOKE THIS POWER OF ATTORNEY IF YOU LATER WISH TO DO SO.

I,_____ , 301 Grey Line Drive, Frackville, PA, 17931, of Schuylkill County, Pennsylvania, do hereby appoint_____(Agent's Name) of (Agent's Address)_____City,_____ _____ZIP Code_____ of_____County, Pennsylvania, as my agent ("my agent") with full power of substitution, for me and in my name, to transact all my business and to manage all my property and affairs as I might do if personally present, including but not limited to exercising the following powers and to act for me in any lawful way with respect to the following initialed subject(s):

INSTRUCTIONS

1. TO GRANT ALL OF THE FOLLOWING POWERS, INITIAL THE LINE IN FRONT OF

   (N) AND IGNORE THE LINES IN FRONT OF THE OTHER POWERS.

2. TO GRANT ONE OR MORE, BUT FEWER THAN ALL, OF THE FOLLOWING POWERS, INITIAL THE LINE IN FRONT OF EACH POWER YOU ARE GRANTING

3. TO WITHHOLD A POWER, DO NOT INITIAL THE LINE IN FRONT OF IT. YOU MAY, BUT NEED NOT, CROSS OUT EACH POWER WITHHELD.

_____ (A) Real estate property transactions

_____ (B) Tangible personal property transactions

_____ (C) Stock and bond transactions

_____ (D) Commodity and option transactions

_____ (E) Banking and other financial institution transactions

_____ (F) Business operating transactions

_____ (G) Insurance and annuity transactions

_____ (H) Estate, trust, and other beneficiary transactions

_____ (I) Claims and litigation

_____ (J) Benefits from Social
Security, Medicare, Medicaid, or other governmental
programs, or civil or military service

_____ (K) Retirement plan
transactions

_____ (M) OTHER

_____ (N) All OF THE
POWERS LISTED ABOVE

YOU NEED NOT INITIAL ANY OTHER LINES IF YOU INITIAL
LINE [N]. ON THE FOLLOWING LINES, YOU MAY GIVE SPECIAL
INSTRUCTIONS LIMITING OR EXTENDING THE POWERS
GRANTED BY YOUR AGENT:

I also revoke any and all previous Powers of Attorney executed
by me.

THIS POWER OF ATTORNEY IS EFFECTIVE IMMEDIATELY AND
WILL CONTINUE UNTIL IT IS REVOKED.

Signed this _____ day of _____ ,20 _____

Commonwealth of Pennsylvania, County of Schuylkill

_____

(Principal Signature)

_____

(Principal Social Security Number)

Sworn to and subscribed before me this_____day of_____, 20_____,

Notary Public,_____

_____

(Witness #1 Sign Name)

_____

(Witness #1 Print Name)

LESSON 3

Becoming Financially Independent From Prison

TAKING CONTROL OF YOUR MONEY

This lesson is the most vital of them all. A bank account is the very foundation upon which all your future success will be built. Without a bank account, it is highly unlikely you'll be able to reach the level of success you want to achieve in prison. If you don't already have control over your money, then it's important that you get control over it now. Your financial success in prison depends on it. Every dollar you own shouldn't be sitting in a prison account controlled by prison administration. Doesn't the DOC already have enough control over your life as it is? I'll answer that - YES. Do you really want them to collect interest off your money, then turning around and tell you how you can spend your own money?

Then there are the strict prison guidelines that inmates are forced to abide by. You know what I'm talking about - the endless order forms and cash slips we have to fill out and submit for approval before the Inmate Accounting Office will process your requested purchase or cut a check for the requested amount of money.

Typically, every day in the life of a prisoner is the same. That's because in prison, your entire day is already planned out for you. Inmates are forced to abide by a strict schedule: we eat at a certain time, go to school and programs at a certain time, go out to the yard and to the gym at a certain time, etc.

As an incarcerated person, there isn't much that is in your control. Therefore, the few important things you are able to control, you should. You have the power to control your energy (who you allow into your circle and befriend).

You're able to control how you spend your time while in prison (you can be as productive as you allow yourself to be) and, most importantly, your money. No one should ever control your money but you!

I'm not saying that there is anything wrong with keeping money in your prison account. Naturally, you're going to want to have money on your books to be able to purchase commissary, sneakers, pay for cable, music, emails, phone time, and everything else you may need money for on the inside. But there is a problem with having every dollar to your name in your prison account. You should never use your prison account as a bank account.

OPENING A BANK ACCOUNT FROM PRISON

There are three ways an inmate can open a bank account from prison:

- Through the prison's resources
- Through your Power of Attorney
- Through direct contact with the bank

Most state prisons provide inmates with some options to open a bank account. However, often these accounts offered through the prisons are limited to small local banks with restrictions and terrible terms. Sure, these accounts can be helpful if you're not able to open an account directly with a more favorable bank, or if you aren't able to find someone to designate as your agent on the streets - at the very least, it will get your money from under the control of the DOC and enable you to have more freedom over how you use your money.

If you decide to go through the prison, the process can easily be initiated by writing to your block counselor. They'll provide you with the options available to you and tell you what you need to do to open the account. But I don't recommend it if you absolutely don't have to and have other options available to you.

It's important to separate your money from the prison as much as possible, even if that means sidestepping the banking options advocated by the DOC. For all we know, the prison administration may get some kind of kickback for every inmate who opens an account with the local bank (which they make our only option to choose from.) And if such a kickback exists, I don't know about you, but I'd rather the prison not get it!

So, in the interest of maximizing your financial independence, I strongly suggest you find someone on the outside - a friend, significant other, family member, or anyone you trust to grant Power of Attorney to. By doing so, you will be authorizing that person to have the power to transact all your business and personal affairs. It will be as if they were actually you out there. And, in a very real sense, they kind of will be.

By law, you're able to grant this person, your Agent, either broad or limited powers. And you'll want to be sure to closely read your state's Uniform Statutory Form/Power of Attorney document so you're fully aware of the rights you'll be vesting over. Yes, your Agent will be legally required to act in your best interests and within your expectations to the extent actually known by your agent, but you will also be authorizing them to act without advance notice to you or prior approval by you. That means, whomever you choose to designate as your Agent, it's very important you keep a detailed record of all your communications with them (emails, letters, etc.) in the event that you need to prove they knew that they weren't acting in accordance with your wishes.

Remember, once you grant someone Power of Attorney and make it official by having it notarized, your first step in attaining financial independence will be to have them open an account on your behalf with a bank, credit union, or an online banking app. Even though the bank account won't be listed on your credit report (of course unless you manage to mess up and owe them money), having an active account suggests to potential lenders that you're financially established. Further, by opening a bank account, you'll be building a relationship with a financial institution, which down the road may very well come in clutch when you're trying to secure a home mortgage, car loan, or any other kind of loan.

CHOOSING THE RIGHT BANK FOR YOU

Now, in opening a bank account, you'll have the option of opening either a checking account, a savings account, or both. The whole idea behind you transferring the majority of your money out of your prison account and into a bank account is not only for you to have complete control over it, but also to maximize all of the perks that you were unable to get from having all your money tied up in a prison account.

I recommend always getting both a savings and a checking account. Even if you may not be in the financial position right now to actually use a savings account, the goal is that in the near future, you'll get to the point where you've earned enough money to be able to start saving.

In addition to opening both types of accounts, you should opt to get a debit card that's linked to your checking account only. You never want to link it to both accounts. In the event you run out of money in your checking account, they will automatically pull money from your savings. Having a bank account along with a debit card allows you to easily control, invest, save, and make purchases with your money from inside prison - using your Agent on the outside.

Here are some things to look for when choosing the right bank:

- No required minimum first deposit
- No required minimum balance
- No monthly fees
- Overdraft protection
- Free debit card replacement
- A credit builder program
- First-time homeowner's mortgage Incentives
- Low APR on loans

Savings vs Checking

To break it down to its simplest form, when it comes to bank accounts, there's two basic types: one for making money and one for spending money.

Savings accounts are technically for making money because they're traditionally interest-bearing accounts, which translates to, the bank pays you for keeping your money there. Now, don't get too excited, because although they pay you, they don't pay much, and there are far better ways for you to put your money to work and have it grow, but that's an entirely different book for you to read once you're back out on the streets.

Checking accounts on the other hand, are basically for spending money using a debit card, wire transfer, bank transfer (from your bank to the business you are paying), and of course - no, they're not obsolete yet - paper checks that you write out by hand.

Here's the thing. Fundamentally, both accounts function the same way. Money goes in, and money goes out, either in the form of cash withdrawals or debit card transactions. So then why should you give a shit which type of account you choose? Because there are different configurations to this basic account setup that include a lot of fine print like fees, limits, and who can use them, it can get confusing. So I'm going to make it easier for you by breaking down the different accounts in plain English.

Basic Checking This is the simplest of the checking accounts to understand because it doesn't do much more than hold your money until you spend it by writing a check or using a debit card. They sometimes have limits on the number of checks you can write a month, and often have a monthly maintenance fee associated with them.

Free Checking If you've ever heard the expression that "nothing is free," then you already know that this most popular type of checking account is not really free.

There are no charges for maintaining the account as long as you stay above an average monthly balance that can range from $100 to several thousand dollars, depending on the bank. The cost of free checking accounts is the money the bank earns by investing your average balance and not sharing the interest with you.

Interest-Bearing Accounts These accounts are often a sort of hybrid in that there is no monthly fee as long as you maintain an average minimum balance. Like with free checking accounts, the bank will then invest your money, and in this case, share some of that interest with you. The catch here is that the required balances are usually too high to make it worth the effort.

Joint Account These accounts can have two or more owners. Typically, married couples would have joint accounts where both spouses have equal access to and responsibility for the account. Whether or not you want to utilize a joint account depends on your relationship and financial goals. These accounts work best when there is open communication between the account holders, so the risk of overdrafts is reduced. I would not suggest this type of checking account.

Express Accounts These accounts can be great for people who have their paychecks directly deposited and seldom venture inside the bank and deal with a teller. The reason is simple: electronic transactions are free, but there is a charge for transactions that involve face-to-face interaction with a teller.

Senior/Junior/Student Account They are available under a variety of names, and their availability is age-dependent, usually under 21 (and a full-time student) or over 55, with retirement as a requirement in some cases. The fees and balance minimums are generally lower on these accounts, which can have other limits on their use to keep the bank's costs down.

Money Markets Like a cross between a savings account and a checking account, these will pay interest on balances over a certain amount and charge fees if the balance is below that amount. The differences are in the rate of interest, usually higher, and the required balance minimums, usually higher. These accounts may also have limits on the number of checks that can be drawn against them each month, usually 3-5.

Online Banking

For some, opening a traditional bank account is not possible until they improve their financial situation, pay down debt, and improve their credit. If you fall into that category, like I once did, there are options that are just as good, sometimes even better, depending on your situation. (I prefer using online banking apps such as Chime and Apple Pay over other traditional banks for my personal finances.) Traditional bank accounts like those offered by Bank of America, TD Bank, Citizens Bank, and Wells Fargo are good. But as an alternative, such as opening an account with a local credit union or an online banking app, are also something to consider.

These days, as everything moves away from brick and mortar and to the Internet, online banks have quickly become popular, especially for the millions of Americans who have bad credit and are deep in debt. That's because these strictly online and app-based banks are typically less restrictive and more accepting of customers with bad financial situations.

Here are some examples of top-trending online banks:

- Chime
- Venmo
- Cash App
- Pay Pal
- Apple Pay
- Google Pay

Like traditional banks, many online banks not only provide many saving and credit- building options, but they also provide you with a physical debit card to make it easy to use your money. (Nowadays, with a banking app, your phone can be used like a debit card with a quick tap against any in-store card reader.)

If you're unable to open either a traditional bank, credit union, or an online bank account, one last option is to load your money onto a reloadable VISA prepaid card. These types of cards can be bought at just about any pharmacy, gas station, or convenience store. Although it's not an ideal situation, anything is better than keeping all your money in a prison account or having all your money in cash once you get out.

Storing your money in a bank account or on a prepaid VISA card allows you to take back control of your finances. By being able to control your money, you're able to maintain your financial independence. You decide what you spend your money on, what to invest in, how much you save, etc. Plus, what if a special occasion comes up and you want to get something for yourself or a loved one? It's easy to do when you're controlling your own money- instead of having to go through the prison's chain of command and filling out forms and cash slips (that can take several days to get approved by the prison administration). It's as easy as having your Agent order the product or service you want.

SAVING MONEY IN PRISON
The 75/25 Budgeting Strategy

I know it's hard to save money while you're incarcerated. Guys often come to me asking for advice on how they can save money and still live comfortably, so I thought I'd take a moment to share a good money-saving strategy that I have been using for years. I call it the 75/25 strategy. It's a simple but effective budgeting principle where you spend only 75% of your monthly income and **save** the remaining 25%. For me, I've always had a difficult time trying to save just because I should - without having a clear target of what I'm actually trying to save up for. And, if you're like me, you'll probably have the same kind of problem, especially when you need every bit of money you've got in your prison account. So, just like I have to do, you need to come up with a specific goal - something that will motivate you to save up for.

Can't think of anything you want to save up for?

I've got one for you. It's a universal target that every state inmate can (and should) have if you can't think of anything specific. Remember, once you are released from prison, you're going to be back out there on your own. Even if you do have a support system willing to help you, the only person who is truly responsible for you is you. And your goal should be to save up as much money as you can right now, when real money is just a luxury, not necessarily a need, so that you can have money when you get out.

Don't ever make the mistake and assume someone else will financially support you or that you're all good because the government will take care of you. People tend to talk a great game to us while we're incarcerated; then, as soon as we come out, they flake out on us.

And, sure, it's a possibility that the government will enroll you in one of its assistance programs, eventually. But let's be real. When have you ever known a government agency to work quickly and efficiently?

Think of it another way. For many of you, you're at a prison that takes a percentage of all your money. For me, in

66

Pennsylvania, they take 25% from the majority of state inmates for ACT 84. In part two of this book, I'll give you the secrets that the DOC certainly doesn't want you to know about. I'll teach you how to actually stop them from taking any more of your money for court costs, fines, and restitution. And though you'll hopefully be successful in stopping the more times than not illegal deductions are being made to your prison account by the prison's Inmate Accounting Office, that shouldn't mean you immediately start spending all of your money and forget about budgeting.

With the extra money you'll hopefully be getting back through my lessons, you'll have a perfect opportunity to deposit those extra dollars into a bank account. Besides, you're already accustomed to getting by without it - so just let it stack up until you get out.

Let's do some quick math.

I've found that the most common amount of money an incarcerated person receives from family and friends is about $50.00 per week. Of course, some get less than that, while there are more fortunate inmates who get more. Don't think too much about the amount. It's just an example.

Okay. So let's just say that you're a PA State inmate, and they used to take 25% of your money for ACT 84. But after reading my book, you've been able to successfully stop them from taking any more of your money and now get 100% of all the money that is deposited to your books. 25% of $50.00 is $12.50. So, because you're already used to spending $37.50 per week, you continue spending the $37.50 every week and put the extra $12.50 right into your savings account.

Although I call this the 75/25 budgeting strategy, because that's what works for me, really, there's no set amount that is ideal. It all depends on what works best for you. Even if it's just 90/10, the important thing is that you at least have something of what you get.

Continuing with the quick math - that $12.50 you save each week turns into $50.00 a month, which then becomes a nice little $600.00 over the course of a year. Really, a little bit more if you include the interest you make, which is laughable, so if you do this for five years, you walk out of prison having saved up a little over $3,000.00. It certainly isn't a whole lot of money - as far as the streets go - but if you spend it wisely, it can definitely help you get back on your feet. And the best part, when you get released and return home, you won't have to rely so much on your support group to help you out!

LESSON 4

"Exposing The Loopholes..."

This lesson is going to be more factual and straight-forward than the others. In it, I am providing the most relevant excerpts from the Fair Credit Reporting Act (FCRA). You're not trying to read the entire Act or decipher it. It's complicated language, so I've gone through it and included only the parts that pertain directly to your ability to dispute and remove unwanted items from your credit report.

In Lesson 5, I'll break down everything in detail. But it's important that you read and have an understanding of the FCRA going into the next Lesson 5. I encourage you to read the contents of this chapter very closely.

In 1996, the FCRA was enacted to ensure that the credit reporting agencies (CRAs) be held accountable for the information they report. The Act was needed because credit reports are known for being full of false and outdated information about consumers. Obviously, the passing of the Act was welcome news for consumers everywhere - finally. The CRAs would be required to start cleaning up their books. Nonetheless, it's still up to people like you and I, the consumers, to avail ourselves of the transparency required by the FCRA. As financially responsible citizens and incarcerated people, it's up to all of us to keep these powerful credit agencies honest. That means we are responsible for keeping ourselves informed about our rights. And that pertains to every aspect in our lives, not only about credit or debt, but everything. If we don't, then we can't be upset or blame anyone except for ourselves when credit reporting agencies, the government, or anyone else exploits the fact that we're not aware of what the law says they can and can't legally do.

In the following lesson, I'll break down what exactly the loopholes in the FCRA are and give you the game plan to use them to your advantage to remove unwanted debt off your credit report. But, right now, here's the shit that you need to know about the Fair Credit Reporting Act, straight from the source.

Section 685, 1681, Obsolete Information Requirements Relating to Information

Section Title here Contained in Consumer Reports

A. Except as authorized under subsection (b) of this section, no consumer reporting agency may make any consumer report containing any of the following items of information:

   i. Cases under Title II or under the Bankruptcy Act that, from the date of entry of the order for relief or the date of adjudication, as the case may be, antedate the report by more than 10 years.

   ii. Civil suits, civil judgments, and records or arrests that, from the date of entry, antedate the report by more than seven years or until the governing statute of limitations has expired, whichever is the longer period.

   Paid tax liens which, from the date of payment, antedate the report by more than seven years.

   iii. Accounts placed for collection or charged to profit and loss that antedate the report by more than seven years.

   iv. Any other adverse item of information, other than records of convictions of crimes, that antedates the report by more than seven years.

B. The provisions of subsection (a) of this section are not applicable in the case of any consumer credit report to be used in connection with:

   1. A credit transaction involving, or which may reasonably be expected to involve, a principal amount of $50,000 • $150,000 or more.

72

2. The underwriting of life insurance involving, or which may reasonably be expected to involve, a face amount of $50,000 • $150,000 or more; or

3. The employment of any individual at an annual salary which equals, or which may reasonably be expected to equal $20,000 • $75,000 or more.

Running of the Reporting Period

1　In General

The seven year period referred to in paragraph (4) and (6) of subsection

(a) shall begin, with respect to any delinquent account that is placed for

collection (internally or by referral to a third party, whichever is earlier), charged to profit and loss, or subjected to any similar action, upon the expiration of the 180-day period beginning on the date of the commencement of the delinquency which immediately preceded the collection activity, charge to profit and loss, or similar action.

2.　Effective Date

Paragraph (1) shall apply only to items of information added to the file of a consumer on or after the date that is 455 days after the date of enactment of the Consumer Credit Reporting Reform Act of 1996.

Information to be Disclosed

Any consumer reporting agency that furnishes a consumer report that contains information regarding any case involving the consumer that arises under Title 11, United States Code, shall include in the report an identification of the chapter of such Title 11 under which such case arises if provided by the source of the information. If any case arising or filed under Title 11, United States Code, is withdrawn by the consumer before a final judgment, the consumer reporting agency shall include in the report that such case or filing was withdrawn upon receipt of documentation certifying such withdrawal.

Indication of Closure of Account by Consumer

If a consumer reporting agency is notified pursuant to Section 623(a)(4)/fcra623.htm-(a)(4) fcra623.htm - (a) (4) that a credit account of a consumer was voluntarily closed by the consumer, the agency shall indicate that fact in any consumer report that includes information related to the account.

Indication of Dispute by Consumer

If a consumer reporting agency is notified pursuant to Section 623(a)(3)/fcra623.htm-(a)(3) fcra623.htm - (a)(3) that information regarding a consumer that was furnished to the agency is disputed by the consumer, the agency shall indicate that fact in each consumer report that includes the disputed information.

Reinvestigations of Disputed Information

1. Reinvestigation Required

a) In general: If the completeness or accuracy of any item of information contained in a consumer's file at a consumer reporting agency is disputed by the consumer and the consumer notifies the agency directly of such dispute, the agency shall reinvestigate free of charge and record the current status of the disputed information, or delete the item from the file in accordance with paragraph (5), before the end of the 30-day period beginning on the date on which the agency receives the notice of the dispute from the consumer.

b) Extension of period to investigate: Except as provided in subparagraph {c), the 30-day period described in subparagraph may be extended for not more than 15 additional days if the consumer reporting agency received information from the consumer during that 30-day period that is relevant to the reinvestigation.

c) Limitations on extension of period to reinvestigate: Subparagraph (b) shall not apply to any reinvestigation in which, during the 30 day period described in subparagraph (a), the information that is the subject of the reinvestigation is found to be inaccurate or Incomplete or the consumer reporting agency determines that the information cannot verified.

2. Prompt Notice of Dispute to Furnisher of Information

a. In general: Before the expiration of the 5-business-day period beginning on the day on which a consumer reporting agency receives notice of a dispute from any consumer in accordance with paragraph {1), the agency shall provide notification of the dispute to any person who provided any item of information in dispute at the address and in the manner established with the person. The notice shall include all relevant information regarding the dispute that the agency has received from the consumer.

b. Provision of other information from consumer: The consumer reporting agency shall promptly provide to the person who provided the information in dispute all relevant information regarding the dispute that is received by the agency from the consumer after the period referred to in subparagraph (a) and before the end of the period referred to in paragraph (I)(a).

3. Determination That Dispute Is Frivolous or Irrelevant

a. In general: Notwithstanding paragraph (1), a consumer reporting agency may terminate a reinvestigation of information disputed by a consumer under that paragraph if the agency reasonably determines that the dispute by the consumer is frivolous or irrelevant, including by reason of a failure by a consumer to provide sufficient information to investigate the disputed information.

b. Notice of determination: Upon making any determination in accordance with subparagraph (a) that a dispute is frivolous or irrelevant, a consumer reporting agency shall notify the consumer of such determination not later than five business days after making such determination, by mail or, if authorized by the consumer for that purpose, by any other means available to the agency.

c. Contents of notice: A notice under subparagraph (b) shall include

I. The reasons for the determination under subparagraph (a); and

II. Identification of any information required to investigate the disputed information, which may consist of a standardized form describing the general nature of such information.

4. Consideration of Consumer Information

In conducting any reinvestigation under paragraph (1) with respect to disputed information in the file of any consumer, the consumer reporting agency shall review and consider all relevant information submitted by the consumer in the period described in paragraph (I)(a) with respect to such disputed information.

5. Treatment of Inaccurate or Unverifiable Information

a) In general: If, after any reinvestigation under paragraph (1) of any information disputed by a consumer, an item of the information is found to be inaccurate or incomplete or cannot be verified, the consumer reporting agency shall promptly delete that item of information from the consumer's file or modify that item of information, as appropriate, based on the results of the reinvestigation.

b) Requirements relating to the reinsertion of previously deleted material:

i. Certification of accuracy of information: If any information is deleted from a consumer's file pursuant to subparagraph (a), the information may not be reinserted in the file by the consumer reporting agency unless the person who furnishes the information certifies that the information is complete and accurate.

ii. Notice to consumer: If any information that has been deleted from a consumer's file pursuant to subparagraph (a) is reinserted in the file, the consumer reporting agency shall notify the consumer of the reinsertion in writing not later than five business days after the reinsertion or, if authorized by the consumer for that purpose, by any other means available to the agency.

iii. Additional information: As part of, or in addition to, the notice under clause (ii), a consumer reporting agency shall provide to a consumer in writing not later than five business days after the date of the reinsertion:

1. A statement that the disputed information has been re-inserted.

2. The business name and address of any furnisher of information contacted and the telephone number of such furnisher, if reasonably available, or of any furnisher of information that contacted the consumer reporting agency in connection with the reinsertion of such information; and a notice that the consumer has the right to add a statement to the consumer's file disputing the accuracy or completeness of the disputed information.

c) Procedures to prevent reappearance: A consumer reporting agency shall maintain reasonable procedures designed to prevent the reappearance in a consumer's file, and in consumer reports on the consumer, of information that is deleted pursuant to this paragraph (other than information that is reinserted in accordance with subparagraph (b)(i).

d) Automated. Reinvestigation system: Any consumer reporting agency that compiles and maintains files on consumers, on a nationwide basis, shall implement an automated system that furnishes information to the consumer reporting agency and may report the results of a reinvestigation. That finds incomplete or inaccurate information in a consumers file to other such consumer reporting agencies.

e) Automated re-investigation system: Any consumer reporting agency that compiles and maintains files on consumers on a nationwide basis shall implement an automated system through which furnishers of information to that consumer reporting agency may report the results of a reinvestigation that finds incomplete or inaccurate information in a consumer's file to other such consumer reporting agencies.

6. Notice of Results of Reinvestigation

a) **In general:** A consumer reporting agency shall provide written notice to a consumer of the results of a reinvestigation under this subsection not later than five business days after the completion of the reinvestigation, by mail or, if authorized by the consumer for that purpose, by other means available to the agency.

b) **Contents:** As part of, or in addition to, the notice under subparagraph (a), a consumer reporting agency shall provide to a consumer in writing before the expiration of the five-day period referred to in subparagraph (a)

i. A statement that the reinvestigation is completed.

ii. A consumer report that is based upon the consumer's file as that file is revised as a result of the re-investigation.

iii. A notice that, if requested by the consumer, a description of the procedure used to determine the accuracy and completeness of the information shall be provided to the consumer by the agency, including the business name and address of any furnisher of information contacted in connection with such information and the telephone number of such furnisher, if reasonably available.

iv. A notice that the consumer has the right to add a statement to the consumer's file disputing the accuracy or completeness of the information; and

v. A notice that the consumer has the right to request under subsection (d) that the consumer reporting agency furnish notifications under that subsection.

7. Description of Reinvestigation Procedure

A consumer reporting agency shall provide to a consumer a description referred to in paragraph (6)(b)(iii) by not later than 15 days after receiving a request from the consumer for that description.

8. Expedited Dispute Resolution

If a dispute regarding an item of information in a consumer's file at a consumer reporting agency is resolved in accordance with paragraph (s)

a. by the deletion of the disputed information by not later than three business days after the date on which the agency receives notice of the dispute from the consumer in accordance with paragraph (l)(a), then the agency shall not be required to comply with paragraphs (2), (6), and (7) with respect to that dispute if the agency:

Provides prompt notice of the deletion to the consumer by telephone.

b. Includes in that notice, or in a written notice that accompanies a confirmation and consumer report provided in accordance with subparagraph (c), a statement of the consumer's right to request under subsection

c. that the agency furnish notifications under that subsection; and Provides written confirmation of the deletion and a copy of a consumer report on the consumer that is based on the consumer's report. If the reinvestigation does not resolve the dispute, the consumer may file a brief statement setting forth the nature of the dispute. The consumer reporting agency may limit such statements to not more than 100 words if it provides the consumer with assistance in writing a clear summary of the dispute.

Whenever a statement of a dispute is filed, unless there are reasonable grounds to believe that it is frivolous or irrelevant, the consumer reporting agency shall, in any subsequent consumer report containing the information in question, clearly note that it is disputed by the consumer and provide either the consumer's statement or a clear and accurate codification or summary thereof.

Following any deletion of information that is found to be inaccurate or whose accuracy can no longer be verified, or any notation as to disputed information, the consumer reporting agency shall, at the request of the consumer, furnish notification that the item has been deleted or the statement, codification or summary pursuant to subsection (b) or (c) of this section to any person specifically designated by the consumer who has within two years prior thereto received a consumer report for employment purposes, or within six months prior thereto received a consumer report for any other purpose, which contained the deleted or disputed information.

LESSON 5

INTRODUCTION

Hood Rich vs Wealthy

What is the difference between being hood rich and being wealthy? Do you know? Maybe you think that there is no actual distinction. That having money is just that and can be called many things. If you think there's no real difference, just two words that mean basically the same thing, then obviously you're neither hood rich nor wealthy, at least not yet anyways.

Someone who is considered to be hood rich almost always deals exclusively in cash money and has the mentality that the more stacks of cash they have the richer they are. And therefore only strives to accumulate more and more cash and foregoes any other financial enterprise that could very well elevate them to the next level of becoming wealthy in the future. This is the concept most people have when they think of a person being hood rich.

However, real wealth is not stacks of cash sitting around waiting to be spent or used to be displayed on social media to showcase a person's status. The biggest difference between a person that's hood rich and a wealthy person is that someone who is wealthy, they don't use cash almost ever. Now, you're probably asking yourself, then how if a wealthy person doesn't use cash can they walk into the finest stores, restaurants, dealerships, and private events and be able to get the best service in the world? The answer is simple.

It's because their wealth speaks not through having an abundance of cash, but through having perfect credit. The very type of credit that I show you how to get in the next lesson. Because of their credit in the minds of all those around them, there every action can be backed up by cash at any time. With perfect credit and money in the bank a wealthy person's signature carries the same value as cash or gold. Now you understand the difference and why Such a person needs never to carry or stack cash.

Take this scenario for a good example. A rich man and a wealthy man walk into the same dealership to buy the same expensive sports car. The rich man dealing only with cash comes in with a bag full of money to cover the cost of the new car where the wealthy man needing no such cash because of his credit walks in with nothing. Needing only his signature the wealthy man completes the entire transaction within a half an hour then drives off in his brand new sports car.

Now on the other side of the dealership the rich man because he is paying for the new car in all cash is having a more lengthy experience. Not only does he have to wait for the dealership to count all the money, but is required to complete additional paperwork for the IRS because he is spending so much cash and spends the rest of the day at the dealership before he can.

Finally drive off and enjoy his brand new sports car.

Now the obvious question is which of the two men would you rather be? You probably would rather be the wealthy man and enjoy all the benefits that comes with having perfect credit. Unlike the person who is hood rich that only has access to the physical money they have and no credit, being wealthy and establishing credit you not only have access to the money you have but you also have access to virtually any amount of money that you want through your credit.

Most people have this common misconception about obtaining credit and they believe that in order to get such a credit reputation takes years of hard work and you must be rich to do so. That's not actually the case. In the following lessons I break down all of the secrets and loopholes in the law that you can use in order to get yourself out of debt and repair your credit score so that you can enjoy all the benefits of a millionaire's credit reputation, without having to be a millionaire!

Secrets to Removing Debt

Your credit history says a lot about you to potential creditors. Hell, even if you don't have a credit history, it says a lot about you. And, sometimes, your credit history says things about you that are outdated, inaccurate, or simply untrue. In fact, it is believed that approximately 50% of all credit reports include false information. Now, I don't know about you, but I think the deck is stacked against us enough. The last thing we need is an inaccurately negative credit report further messing up our lives.

But there's good news. Because of the Fair Credit Reporting Act, (FCRA), as discussed in the previous lesson, your credit history can be changed if you know what to do. It's even possible to get legitimate negative items taken off your credit report as well. This happens when a credit reporting agency (CRA) is unable to verify the information on your credit report within the 30-day period allowed by the FCRA. Remember, the FCRA allows you the right to dispute anything on your credit report - and, like I said, yes, that means you're even allowed to dispute accurate information. The burden of proof is not on you but on the CRA to demonstrate that the contents of your credit report are actually true. They have to do the legal work. Not you.

In this lesson, I'm going to break down the loopholes of the FCRA for you so that you can get outdated, inaccurate, and untrue items expunged from your credit report. And just maybe you'll even be able to get legitimate items removed, too.

It is time for class.

How to Dispute Your Credit Report

Okay. So the Fair Credit Reporting Act (FCRA) is a typical bureaucratic mishmash of strange and complicated language that requires a damn finance degree to understand. Personally, I think they write that shit like that on purpose because they don't want any of us normal people to be able to make sense of it all. But, no worries, I got you.

For our purposes here, there's only one thing you need to know: The credit reporting agencies Equifax, TransUnion, and Experian - have only 30 days to investigate and resolve your dispute once it's made. That's the key. Because here's the thing: It's all but impossible for the CRA to get in touch with every party included in your claim and settle the dispute within that 30-day window - especially if you lodge a claim via certified mail instead of electronically (because mailing gives them an even smaller window of time to investigate). If they are unable to respond to you within 30 days with proof (your signature consenting to the debt), then the CRA is in violation of the Fair Credit Reporting Act. That means they'll be in default, making them liable to civil suits for Enablement of Identify Fraud, Defamation, and a bunch of other charges.

By pressing the CRA to get in touch with you by mail, you're not letting them have any extra time to conduct their investigation. That means, almost as a matter of course, they'll have to expunge the negative item from your credit report. When the CRA does not contact you to resolve the issue within 30 days, then a few weeks later, they'll send you a letter informing you that the item you disputed has been removed. And here's the kicker- if one CRA removes an item from your credit report, the other agencies typically will as well.

Types of Disputes

Generally, there are three primary types of disputes you can file.

1. Disputing False Information

Okay. So let's imagine that your credit report says you owned a Tesla back in 2015. Nice car. You must have been doing your thing out there. But the problem is, you never actually owned a Tesla. It could be that someone stole your identity, or it may just be the credit reporting agency made a mistake. It happens all the time, but don't worry. You can do something about it.

That's why they came up with the Fair Credit Reporting Act. It gives you the right to contact CRA directly and dispute this item. Of course, they will still have the 30 days to conduct their investigation, and in this instance, it shouldn't be a problem at all because the CRA won't be able to confirm the information, and by law, they will have to remove it from your credit file.

2. Disputing Outdated Information

Now, let's say you really did own a Tesla in 2015, but it ended up being repossessed. Sure, it might be true. But the law states that items can only stay on your credit report for no more than seven years. The same Statute of Limitations that applies to most criminal charges also applies to your credit. After seven years, the items must be removed, just like with most criminal charges. There are exceptions with credit. The only things that can legally stay on your credit report longer than seven years is a bankruptcy and student loans. But unlike student loans, which remain on your credit file until they're paid off, bankruptcies can only stay on for ten years.

3. Disputing Accurate Information, Unable to be Confirmed

This is the loophole that I teach you about in this lesson and why the FCRA can be such a powerful tool for you: Nowhere does it say you can't dispute legitimate debt that's being reported on your credit report. Most people just automatically assume that you can't, because if you do, you'll get in trouble. Little do they know that's not the case at all. The law only specifies that the credit reporting agencies have 30 days to verify the information you're disputing - and if they can't verify it within 30 days with proof of your original signature, then the item must be expunged.

Keeping with the example of the Tesla that was repossessed, but now instead of 2015, it happened much more recently, in 2023. This scenario is bad for two reasons: Obviously, because it's true, but also because it happened within the last seven years. That means a record of this repossession has every right to show up on your credit report.

But, because of the FCRA, you're still allowed to dispute it. And by lodging your dispute through the mail, you'll be giving the CRA such a limited window of time to conduct their investigation that it's likely they could just expunge the item by default, because, if they don't, they're opening themselves up to a civil lawsuit.

This is what makes the FCRA so great. The responsibility isn't on you, the consumer, but on the Credit Reporting Agency to prove their own records. The FCRA was put into law because credit reports are notoriously inaccurate. Every month, there are literally billions of items added to and removed from the CRA records, so it's only natural that there are errors.

The Game Plan

Follow this process to dispute items on your credit report:

1. Request copies of your credit report.

2. Thoroughly examine the reports.

- First, I would look for anything that is inaccurate. This can even be seemingly harmless mistakes
- Closed accounts that show as open, or open accounts that show as closed
- Bankruptcies that aren't labeled by their chapter number
- Inaccurate account numbers
- Inaccurate or misspelled address, phone number, name, Social Security number, etc.
- Inaccurate liens
- Genuinely false information, such as accounts that aren't yours or payments listed as late that weren't late at all
- Anything more than seven years old

For instance, let's say you had several past due payments on a loan. And, on your credit report, the CRA correctly listed you as the account holder, but one of the digits is wrong in your Social Security number. Even though it's your account and, yes, you missed several payments, you're absolutely allowed to dispute that item. Further, you're not required to tell the credit bureau what your actual Social Security number is, only that the Social Security number listed is not yours. Because they made a minor mistake, they won't be able to confirm it, and they'll have to expunge the item from your record.

3. How to Dispute the Items

You'll need to write a letter to the credit bureau detailing clearly what you're disputing and why you're disputing it. Regardless of the listing, it is essential to state that you are disputing its accuracy. It's not a lie. If you have nothing particular to dispute, simply say you're challenging the accuracy. Personally, I suggest you challenge everything. Who knows? They might not be able to verify it in time.

4. Use Certified Mail

You're going to need evidence of when you mailed the letter, so you'll be able to show when the 30-day timeline started. Also, be smart and make a copy of the letter for your own files!

5. Be Patient

As you should know by now, credit reporting agencies have 30 days to investigate each listing you challenge. If they're unable to verify it, the listing must be expunged. No confirmation means an expunged item - It's that simple, no matter how true it is. If they fail to remove the item, you can file a civil suit for violating the FCRA (and get paid!) and you can report them to the Federal Trade Commission.

Ultimately, even if it doesn't work out the way you'd hoped, you're still allowed to dispute the items over and over again, forcing the credit reporting agencies to conduct investigation after investigation. If, during one of these investigations, they fail to get back to you within 30 days, you'll have succeeded.

Tip: Sometimes credit bureaus decline to investigate or remove challenges to "hard inquiries."

A hard inquiry is when a money lender pulls your credit report (usually when you apply for a loan) to see whether you are creditworthy. Instead, the CRA might tell you that the hard inquiry is just "a statement of fact." That's incorrect, and it could be a potentially costly mistake for them. The FRCA requires that all challenged items must be investigated, including hard inquiries. If a credit bureau declines to investigate hard inquiries, (as sometimes they do), you can sue them for $1,000 each time and win!

Finally, if there are still listings on your credit report that you can't get removed but still wish to dispute, then according to the FCRA, you're allowed to write a 100-word explanation to portray your point of view about the listing. The CRA is required to furnish a copy of your statement to any potential creditor who goes to pull your report.

All right. That's about all there is to it. Yes, a lot of the things we've talked about here might seem like nothing more than exploiting technicalities. And, depending on your situation, that might be exactly what you're trying to do. So, before you go and have a crisis of conscience on me, I've got one thing to ask: How many times have you been screwed by a technicality before... Exactly. So I don't see much of a problem in exploiting some of the few technicalities that exist for our benefit.

To dispute any inaccuracies on your Equifax credit report, please send – via U.S. Mail - this form along with copies of the items below in order to verify your information and address. To ensure that your request is processed accurately, please enlarge copies of any items that contain small print (i.e. driver's license, W2 Forms, etc.). Copies that are not legible or contain highlighting may cause us to request that you resubmit your request for clarity. You can also submit disputes online at myequifax.com.

Identification Information

First Name   Last Name   Middle Initial   Suffix

Current Address   City   State   Zip

Former Address   City   State   Zip

SSN   Date of Birth

       M M   D D   Y Y Y Y

Proof of Identity
(check box for and include a copy of one of the following)

     Social Security Card
     Pay stub with Social Security Number
     W2 or 1099 Form

The item you select must contain your SSN

Proof of Address
(check box for and include a copy of one of the following)

     Driver's license or state identification card
     Rental lease agreement/house deed
     Pay stub with address
     Utility or phone bill (gas, electric, water, cable, mobile)

The item you select must contain your current mailing address

If your identity information differs from the information listed on your credit report, please provide a copy of your driver's license, social security card, or recent utility bill that reflects the correct information.

Complete, Print, and send (via U.S. mail) this form along with the requested documents to the following address:

Equifax Information Services LLC
P.O. Box 740256
Atlanta, GA 30374

FRAUD/IDENTITY THEFT VICTIM

     Please check this box if you are disputing items on your credit report that you suspect to be fraudulent or a result of identity theft.

If you have a Police Report, FTC Identity Theft Report, or Affidavit of Fraud documenting fraud/identity theft, please include a copy with this request.

Dispute Personal Information (Is any of the information below incorrect on your credit report? If not, leave blank.)

Date of Birth (Which is incorrect)   Phone Number (Which is incorrect?)

   M M   D D   Y Y Y Y
Social Security Number (Which is incorrect?)   Employers (Which are incorrect?)

Names (Which are incorrect?)

Addresses (Which are incorrect?)

SAMPLE CREDIR LETTER 1

SMART COMMUNICATIONS/PADOC

P.O. BOX 33028

ST. PETERSBURG, FLORIDA 33733

DATE _____

SOCIAL SECURITY# _____

CONFIRMATION# _____

DATE OF BIRTH _____

TO:

_____

_____

_____

I received my annual free credit report and I discovered (_) negative account(s) that you have open under my SSN# that I wish to challenge the accuracy, compliance, and reportability of the account(s) in question are listed below:

- _____ account# _____

- _____ account# _____

Ask for your company to please open up an investigation and validate all of the information of the above-listed creditor(s) and provide me with physical copies of any such documentation bearing my signature to prove the account(s) are in fact mine. Without true verification of the legitimacy of these account(s) I will have no other choice except to proceed as if I have been a victim of identity Theft and all the above-listed account(s) that your company reported on my credit file opened fraudulently without my knowledge or permission.

THEREFORE, I formally request that all of these account(s) be immediately removed from my credit file. Please note, you have 30 days to complete the investigation as per the Fair Credit Reporting Act section 611 (a) (1) (A). I am keeping a careful record of your actions, timeline, and METHOD OF VERIFICATION.

FURTHER, I DO NOT CONSENT TO E-OSCAR OR TO ANY OTHER MEANS OF AUTOMATED VERIFICATION.

Failure to respond satisfactorily within 30 days of receipt of this certified letter may result in a small claims action against your company seeking $1,000 per violation.

1. Defamation

2. Negligent Enablement of Identity Fraud

3. Violation of the Fair Credit Reporting Act.

Cc: Consumer Financial Protection Bureau

Cc: Attorney General's Office

Cc: Better Business Bureau

SAMPLE CREDIT LETTER 2

[Credit Reporting Agency's Name]

[Credit Reporting Agency's Address]

[City, State, Zip Code]

Dear Credit Bureau,

I received a copy of my credit report and I have found that in accordance to the FCRA, you violated my rights under 15 U C.1681 SECTION 602 WHICH STATES A CONSUMER REPORTING AGENCY CANNOT FURNISH AN ACCOUNT WITHOUT MY WRITTEN INSTRUCTIONS Pursuant to 15 USC 1666b, A creditor may not treat a payment on a credit card account under an open dash end consumer credit plan as late for any purpose, unless the creditor has adopted. Reasonable procedures designed to ensure that each periodic statement, including the information required by section 1637(b) of this title, is mailed or delivered to the consumer not later than 21 days before the payment due date.

I NEVER gave you, OR the above listed creditors, any written instructions. To furnish any information on my consumer report that is in violation of 15 USC 1681b. Credit reporting agency has caused severe stress and anxiety due to the abusive and unfair practices.

LIST LATE PAYMENTS HERE (ACCOUNT NAME AND MONTH/YEAR OF LATE PAYMENT)

- _____
- _____
- _____

You should be ashamed of yourself for ASSUMING this role and position to constantly commit fraud and cause harm to consumers! These accounts are listed with late or missed payments, and that is incorrect. According to the provisions of the Fair Credit Reporting Act, I demand that these items be investigated and removed.

DUE TO THESE VIOLATIONS OF MY CONSUMER RIGHTS, I AM DEMANDING THAT YOU UPDATE THE ABOVE LISTED LATE PAYMENTS AS "OK" OR "PAID AS AGREED"

Best regards,

(Full Name)

SAMPLE CREDIT LETTER 3

Full Name

Social Security Number

Date of Birth

Current Mailing Address

To whom it may concern:

I just received a copy of my credit report and found several inaccurate items that I wish to challenge. They are:

1. To bank Visa account xxxx-xxxx-xxxx-xx, state. That this account was paid 30 days late period. I have never been late on this account.

2. American Express Account xxxx-xxxx-xxxx-xx. State this account was charged off. I don't agree and challenge the accuracy of this claim.

3. Big Bob's Used Cars: I have never had a loan with them.

In addition, you list 2 accounts that are more than 7 years old period. Pursuant to the FCRA, all credit older than seven years must be removed from my report.

Home Depot xxxx-xxxx-xxxx-xx

Amazon Acct xxxx-xxxx-xxxx-xx

I appreciate your looking into these discrepancies on my report.

(sign your name)

LESSON 6

Introduction

There are many different strategies and ways you can choose to deal with the shittier aspects of life as well as yourself, and of course, there are right ways, and there are wrong ways to do so, but more times than not, There is a fine line between the two that is almost never definitively clear. Therefore, when faced with having to make the choice of how you will deal with all of your problems, and all the bad shit that life will throw at you. It is usually chosen by what actually feels right to you, rather than what society says is right. Most importantly, it is whether you have it in you to put the work in and do it the hard way, or if you don't, and just want to do it the easiest way possible.

That one choice, as insignificant as it may seem at the time, has the power to affect the rest of your life, because whatever way you end up choosing, is how you will deal with everything. Usually for the rest of your life, or like me, for a better part of it. So I hope you can understand how choosing the wrong way can have such a powerful effect on your future! Although they are contributing factors, it is not necessarily what you did, how you did it, or who you did it too, that actually defines you as a person. You only think that because that is exactly what society uses to judge whether you are good or bad, and they really shouldn't it's not fair.

How I see it, you can't judge a person solely off of what they have done, because. Let's be honest, everyone throughout their lifetime make just as many good decisions as bad ones, and makes three times as many mistakes than both combined. So it really comes down to the choices that we make in life, and not what we have done, that truly defines us. Things like how you decide to handle yourself when faced with having to deal with bad feelings, difficult emotions, and overwhelming urges. Will you choose the way that requires hard work, or will you take the easy way out and risk fucking up the rest of your life by doing so!

For me, I obviously chose the wrong way. As with everything in life, I never wanted to work for or put any effort into anything at all. The choice I made was simple. I chose to deal with it the easiest way possible, which of course I had no way of knowing at the time, nor would I have probably even cared if I had known, that by choosing to suppress everything and just never deal with anything. However, I inadvertently started the countdown to my very own self destruction! As you can imagine, because of who I am and how fucked up I had been, especially as a teenager, I had made every aspect of my upbringing that much more impossibly difficult than it ever needed to be.

My whole entire adolescent life, my family, the few actual friends that I had, my grades as well as my bad behavior at school, both my mental and physical health, just about everything back then had been affected. In the worst possible way, by how I was dealing with all of my problems, which I really wasn't dealing with any of my emotions or problems, and instead, pretended that they did not exist. By doing so, I didn't realize just how much it was actually affecting me or the fact that every day I was becoming more and more fucked up because of it. And because of this, like everything else, I kept my feelings and problems that I was struggling with all to myself believing if I didn't say anything, it would eventually go away. Never asking for help because then it would make it real.

No one, including myself, knew how to help me. Because no one, not even my parents, knew the full extent of my problems or that I was struggling so hard to figure out how to control all of the absolute chaos happening within myself. All anyone knew was what I projected, which was a pissed off, stubborn, troubled kid who constantly got in trouble, blew up and acted out with very little to no provocation.

For me, the coping mechanism of suppressing my more difficult emotions and feelings came to me when I was only a young kid. While I was going through some traumatic events both in my life, with my parents getting divorced. And inside my head with all of the psychological and emotional problems I was struggling with because of how fucked up I was. I couldn't possibly deal with it all, even if I had wanted to, which I didn't.

So, as you can imagine, when I learned that I could actually cope by not having to deal with any of the shit that I was going through. And continue living my life as if none of my problems even existed. I jumped at the opportunity to live my life like that. However like anything that is easy and seems to be too good to be true, it usually comes with negatives that you may not realize until it's too late. Just like how not dealing with and forever suppressing everything seems like such a obvious way to cope with the hard realities that is life.

The thing with this whole concept is that it starts out so unbelievably great, like a weight has been lifted off you that you didn't even know was weighing you down. It's the best feeling of your entire life once you are no longer burdened by any of your problems, emotions, or pain. Sound familiar? Like anything that is easy and immediately gratifying, however, it never stays that way for long and ends up hurting us way more than it actually helps us. Think of it as a big ass, warm and cuddly bear coming up behind you and wrapping his arm around you, and you instantly Feel so safe, protected, and comfortable. The feeling is so amazing and powerful that you don't want it to ever stop. So what do you do? Absolutely nothing. You let the bear stay right there, hugging you. And you don't even think about fighting the bear off. You enjoy the feeling the bear gives you so much, you keep the bear around for years and by doing so, you don't even realize that you have become dependent on that bear.

You can't imagine your life now without having the bear to make you feel good, because why would you ever want to not feel so good, right? Then one day, out of nowhere as the bear has its big, soft, furry arms around you, making you feel all warm and safe, just as it has for years, all of a sudden the bear snaps and turns against you. It is so quick that you never see it coming as he uses his arms to rip your fucking head right off your shoulders, killing you instantly! As easy as not dealing with your problems and pretending that they don't exist can bring you immediate great feelings of unburdened happiness, it can as easily do the complete opposite of that and cause great pain and suffering, even destroying your entire life in the blink of an eye. Just like the bear, you will never see it coming until it's too late!

It's not lost on me, that the bear analogy could easily be used to describe the feeling of using drugs, and how something that makes you feel so good could end you so quickly. With addiction, even knowing the serious risks of using drugs, we would rather continue to use and feel good, ignoring life and all of our problems, rather than be safe and stop using and feel alone and exposed to everything that we have been desperately trying to avoid. Why do you think that drugs are the natural next progression for people that are just as fucked up as I am? Because drugs for people like me are totally different from what normal people use them for, which is recreation. Sure, I have fun and enjoy getting high, absolutely, but for me, drugs are much more than just that, they are a better and more powerful coping mechanism when I have exhausted all other conventional methods of dealing with my problems.

Like anything in life, after a while, whatever it is that you are doing to help yourself, whether it is medicine, meditation, or some inner psychological process. For example, never dealing with any difficult emotions or feelings, and burying them deep, and going on living, pretending as if they don't exist. I'll admit that it works great for a while, but eventually, it loses its power over time and begins to slowly taper off until it no longer works at all. That is true with everything that pertains to psychology and your mental health. It doesn't matter what it is. Nothing is ever a permanent solution to your problems it is all only temporary until the next solution.

I have talked about my struggle with not wanting to deal with my problems or anything for that matter, starting at a young age. I have talked about how much coping that way fucked me up and put me on a path of self-destruction that directly caused me to live such an unnecessarily difficult life. There is however, one more effect that I have not yet talked about and need to because it has consumed such a big part of my life. It is probably the most relevant problem that most parolees struggle with, more so than anything else, and that's addiction.

I could literally write an entire book on addiction, but there are far too many of those that have already been written, so I am just going to keep it about me and my experience with addiction and how it had a direct effect on the type of mindset I've had. I'll start by answering the one question everyone always asked me: what made me start using drugs? I don't have some crazy story as to how I started using drugs. Nothing is unique about it. In fact, my story is probably very similar to every single one of your own original stories. The way I tried drugs to fit in and try to seem cool. But my reason for continuing to use had nothing to do with the peer pressure or keeping up appearances, and everything to do with having found a much better and even easier way to cope with everything.

If you're anything like me, then you understand every day is a struggle because everything that we experience is 10 times of what a normal person experiences, especially when we are sober. Our impulses, feelings, anger, mood swings, everything about us is so much more intense than normal people. We tend to love faster and harder than normal people. We hold on to grudges longer, and our anger is on a whole other level.

We are the same as addicts in the respect that we have to work extra hard every minute, every hour, taking it one day at a time to control our impulses, anger, self-destructive behavior, everything, or else we will give in and do something fucked up that we are certain to regret later. It's just like an addict giving in to their desire to get high and relapsing. It never gets better. It never goes away. We are stuck having to live with it for the rest of our lives. And always, where one moment of weakness, one bad decision away from doing something that will potentially fuck up our life even more than it already is.

That is why most of us become addicts in the first place, even though we have to deal with more problems than a normal addict has to, even without drugs, So it makes no sense as to why we would put ourselves through dealing with even more shit. The answer is simple. We find solace in drugs because they help us cope better than anything else, even if it is just for a brief moment of instant gratification. Then again, when you're like us, instant gratification is our biggest weakness. It's our kryptonite.

Although everybody says things like, it's never too late, or better late than never, in reality, that is just bullshit, and anyone who tells you that damn well knows it is. The only reason they are saying it to you, is because you've already fucked up and took way too long to figure out whatever it was that you were doing wrong. And even if after you have finally fixed everything, it doesn't matter, because you can't undo all the damage that has already been done, and they know it, even if you don't. Of course, it took me until just recently to realize everything that I have done so incredibly wrong, including the hard fact that there is no such thing as "never too late." Because of that, I have spent the better part of my life dealing with things with a completely wrong mindset, and acting like an asshole towards everyone, especially those closest to me.

I have fucked my life up to the point of no return. It's a difficult thing to have to accept, to know that if I had just pulled my stubborn head out of my ass and realize that what I was doing was destroying me. If I had changed a long time ago, I would have had a chance at being able to salvage what was still left of my fucked up life. It may be too late for me now to make any real changes in my life at this point. My advice don't be like the teenage version of me who was pissed off at the world and stubborn to the point of stupidity. I was incapable of accepting help or listening to reason. Seriously, don't wait until it's too late and you've finally hit your absolute rock bottom, fucked your whole life up and lost everything and everyone. Don't wait until it's too late before you finally decide enough is enough and you want to start actually putting the work into bettering yourself. Because if you do you might find that it's too late.

Secrets To Improving Your Credit Score

As an incarcerated person, it is incredibly important for you to start taking steps now, while inside, to repair your credit. Because you're in jail, this might seem like an impossible task, I know, I've been where you are and have had the same negative thoughts: I'm powerless in here; there's nothing I can do; I'll just deal with all that shit when I get out, etcetera. Thoughts like this might be comforting at first. If we believe in our own helplessness, then we don't feel so bad about not working to attend to our financial situation. Besides, when you're locked down, such concerns like "credit scores" don't seem all that important.

But having been incarcerated and then released several times, I know from first-hand experience that it's never too early to start rebuilding your credit, because, if you're like 90% of prisoners out there, you will be released back into society one day, and you need to do everything within your power to set yourself up for success when that day comes. Having good credit is super-important when it comes to renting an apartment, getting reasonably priced car insurance, and obtaining loans needed for large purchases. Also, good credit scores can help you get more favorable interest rates, credit cards, and even better employment opportunities. It shows banks and landlords that you're a trustworthy person who takes their finances seriously.

I know it might sound unbelievable, but trust me, it's absolutely possible to rebuild your credit from behind bars if you start taking steps now. You can start laying the groundwork for an easier transition back into society and set yourself up for tremendous financial health down the road. I mean, really, what else are you doing with your time?

Obstacles in Repairing Your Credit Score From Prison

Nothing worth doing is ever easy. I can't tell you how many times my parents told me that as a kid. Honestly, it was kind of annoying. But now, I understand what they were trying to do - they were trying to instill in me an awareness that, if I wanted to achieve anything in life, it was going to take work.

Today, I am 32 years old, and I'm every bit as stubborn as I was back then. But I've also reached a point in my life where I'm finally able to recognize the wisdom in that lesson. And if you've decided you're going to start repairing your credit while in prison, you, too, will have to accept the fact that it's going to take a bit of work. But I've done the research for you, and if you're willing to do the work, the benefits for your future will be well worth it.

I probably don't need to tell you this, but the obstacles prisoners face can, at first, seem pretty daunting. To overcome these obstacles, it's important to be conscious of the hoops you'll have to jump through. Here are some of the most well- known challenges unique to prisoners when it comes to rebuilding credit from the inside:

- **Inadequate Financial Education:** If you're in prison, it's likely your life hasn't been all sunshine and silver spoons. A lot of people who are locked up don't even have a GED, let alone a college degree. Also, you might not have had the best role models as parents, parents who held your hand as they walked you through life's difficulties, so you probably were never exposed to the financial education held by trust fund kids.

- **Collecting/Making Payments and Handling Finances:** Being in prison can seriously get in the way of your ability to collect and make payments and handle your finances, particularly if you're dependent upon help from someone on the streets, but that's okay. Later in this chapter, we'll talk about what you can do to set up dependable avenues for collecting payments and appointing a trustworthy friend or family member to handle your finances, pay your bills, and even keep an eye on your all-important credit reports.

- **Minimal Communication Access:** Unless you're in some crazy, low-security club fed, you probably have minimal access to phones, the Internet, and your banking resources. This can present a whole host of difficulties when it comes to staying on top of your finances.

- **Minimal Access to Credit Building Opportunities:** Repairing your credit usually means you'll need access to such financial resources as loans and credit cards. But, in prison, as discussed above, you likely have limited access to these financial resources. But take a deep breath. In the pages to come, we'll go over various specific ways inmates can repair their credit with special programs and secured credit cards.

- **Rising above these obstacles means** you'll have to be proactive, creative, and focused. But if you use the resources around you, work to perform healthy credit-building methods, and aren't too proud to ask for help when you need it, you'll be amazed by just how much you can achieve from behind bars.

- **From where you're sitting now, dealing with dick-** head guards and a prison administration that doesn't believe in you, you might find it hard to imagine there are ways to improve your financial literacy while incarcerated, but you're going to have to get out of that negative mindset - because if you're willing to take some initiative, there really are things you can do to upgrade your level of financial intelligence. Here are some of the basic resources available to nearly all inmates:

- **Organizations on the Streets:** There are countless organizations on the streets like nonprofits and financial foundations, which extend educational opportunities to inmates through things like workshops and correspondence courses. Yeah, it's going to be annoying to have to mail out your work and wait for it to be sent back. But a lot of these correspondence courses are free because institutions like banks and money lenders actually want people to be financially literate. And they know that, even though you're incarcerated right now, you'll one day be a potential customer, so don't be afraid to write to a company that offers correspondence courses on financial literacy. It might even help your cause when you see the parole board because they like to see it when prisoners proactively take steps toward rehabilitation, right?

- **Prison Programs:** Most prisons offer financial education courses with the goal of rehabilitation and facilitating re-entry. These classes might seem to you bogus nonsense prisoners use for public relations purposes, but if you give them a chance - and really listen to what's being taught you might learn something. Like anything else, you're going to get out what you put in, so pay attention! These courses often teach you valuable information about handling your credit, how to budget, and how to achieve financial goals.

- **Prison Library:** The prison library is a great place to start if you want to do some research on your own. Most institutional libraries have tons of magazines, books, and other educational information you can use to grow your knowledge and build the practical skills that will advance your financial success in the future.

- **Online Courses:** If you're lucky enough to have a friend or family member on the streets who's willing to help, have them do some research for you about what online programs offer courses in financial education, specifically courses about repairing credit. You may not have access to the Internet, but your friends and family do. Don't be afraid to ask them to print off that material and send it to you through the mail. I know money's tight for you in prison, but a lot of these courses are inexpensive or even free.

By exploring and immersing yourself in financial education options, you can improve your financial knowledge and essential skills for repairing your credit. Keep in mind, education is your most important weapon, enabling you to make sound financial choices and in paving the way to financial success upon your release.

All right. I'll stop beating around the bush. If you're reading this, then you want the facts, not just some generic advice about going to the library and taking classes while in prison. Let's get into it. Here are some of the most effective ways to repair your credit from behind bars.

- **Capitalize on Someone Else's Good Credit:** You probably knew spoiled rich kids when you were growing up, whose parents gave them credit cards? Yeah, those kids were douchebags, I know. But their parents were pretty smart, because these rich kids didn't actually have their own credit cards. It's much more likely that their parents added them as "an authorized user" on their own account. As authorized users, those kids had joint access to their parents' line of credit as well as their credit history, meaning their parents' good credit habits were reflected in the douchebag's credit score. Basically, those rich kids were developing good credit because they were benefiting from the fact that their rich parents always paid the balance.

  But here's the thing: Their parents could also have simply added their spoiled kids as authorized users, yet never actually had given them a credit card - and these kids still would've been establishing good credit because the parents would still be paying off their own balance every month. And this payment history would still show up on the kids' credit reports.

So here's my question: Why leave this trick only to the rich kids? You, as an incarcerated adult, can do the same thing. If you have a friend or family member with good credit, try asking them if they'd be willing to add you to their account as an authorized user. If they're wary because of your criminal past, let them know that they don't really have to give you access to an authorized user card. Simply by adding you to their account as a joint user, your credit score will benefit from their positive credit habits.

However, be mindful! By using their credit to establish credit of your own means, they'll be putting a lot of faith in you, especially when you get out. If you fail to live up to that faith, you can destroy not only your own credit but theirs as well. And perhaps even worse, you could ruin your relationship with that person, so do not take this responsibility lightly.

- **Get a Secured Credit Card:** If you currently have bad credit and are trying to repair it, banks may be wary of offering you a line of credit. They'd rather trust someone who has no credit than trust someone trying to repair their credit. But don't worry. Instead of getting a conventional credit card, you can apply for something called a "secured" credit card. Secured credit cards provide a great credit-building opportunity with minimal risk to financial institutions. This type of credit card is called "secured" because you will be required to open a savings account and make a deposit with the issuing bank. Generally, the amount you deposit will determine how much credit they extend to you. For example, if you deposit $200, the bank will extend you a $200 credit limit. Your initial deposit will serve as collateral. This means that if you use the secured credit card to make a purchase but fail to pay the debts, the bank can use your initial $200 deposit to cover the debt. Your initial deposit lessens the risk for the issuing institution, making it easier for people with bad credit or no credit to get approved.

Here are some important factors to consider when it comes to choosing a secured credit card:

The Interest Rate: Secured credit cards can come with interest rates running from 10% on the low end all the way to 20% on the high end. It goes without saying that you're going to want the lowest interest rate you can find.

The Deposit Requirements: Typically, the minimum deposit required is about $200, but it's up to the bank. And you can always deposit more. If you do decide to deposit more, you'll have a higher credit limit. For example, a $600 initial deposit will usually give you a $600 credit limit.

Fund Matching: Some banks will even match your deposit, extending you extra credit. For instance, if you deposit $200, some banks will extend to you a $400 credit limit.

Grace Period: If you're going to become a more financially intelligent person, you'll need to familiarize yourself with grace periods. This is the window of time in which you're allowed to pay off your balance without incurring extra charges. Most grace periods can be anywhere from 0 to 30 days. You're going to want the longest grace period possible, just in case.

Can It Become Unsecured: You'll find it's a lot quicker and easier to establish really good credit with a conventional, unsecured credit card. Some secured credit cards let you trade in your secured card for an unsecured card after a certain amount of timely payments. It usually takes about a year. When that happens, you'll get your initial deposit back.

You will need to determine which of these considerations matters the most to you. Also, you'll need to ensure, with whatever secure card you choose, that the issuing lender reports your payment history to the three major credit bureaus: Experian, TransUnion, and Equifax. If it doesn't, you won't be repairing your credit at all.

Another important thing you'll need to check into is whether your issuing lender reports your card as "secured" to the credit bureaus. It's better if your lender reports your card as unsecured. This is because when a secured card is reported as unsecured, potential creditors can't tell the difference when they read your credit report. And these potential lenders will be more likely to issue you an unsecured line of credit if it looks like you already have unsecured credit.

Get a Secured Loan to Diversify Your Credit: Secured loans, sometimes called "passbook" loans, are very similar to secured credit cards. The gist is the same, it's just carried out differently. Here's how it works: Open up a savings account at a bank. Every few weeks, add some money to the account. After several months, ask the bank for a loan, but make sure you ask for an amount that's less than the amount in your account and secured by the funds you already have. Because the loan will be secured by your account, the bank will loan you the money. Just like that, you'll have induced a major bank to extend you a loan, and it likely won't be reported as a "secured" loan either.

Here's a tip: It's important to have a healthy mix of credit to repair your credit score - credit cards, loans, mortgages, etcetera. The more different types of credit you have (and pay down consistently), the more likely you'll be to build a great credit score.

DRIP: If you want to get crazy, you can also look into getting a credit card from a gasoline company. Usually, you'd need to have really good credit to do this, but there's a loophole.

First, you'll need to choose a publicly traded oil company, preferably one you (or your family) pass by often. The secret is that you have to have someone on the streets, probably the person you've designated as your power of attorney, purchase stock in the gas company. Have them call the gas company and say you'd like to join their dividend reinvestment plan (DRIP). Whatever you do, don't have whoever does it say they want to apply for a credit card. FYI, you'll have to purchase, at the very least, $250 worth of stock to qualify for the company's DRIP.

Once you've bought the stock and been enrolled in the company's DRIP for a few months, they'll send you an application for a gas credit card. Really, it's a lot like a secured credit card, but with a DRIP, the card will be "secured" by the stock you bought. And a bonus: they're reported as unsecured to the credit bureaus.

Okay, so there's the game plan. The advice I've laid out here might seem super simple, but here's the thing - it is. Too often, we tend to overcomplicate things just because we don't understand how they work. However, repairing your credit doesn't need to be rocket science. If you're willing to educate yourself and try some of the steps I mentioned above, you can absolutely empower yourself with all the benefits that come with having good credit.

Here are a few general tips that you should understand to help you along the way:

1. Making Timely Payments: Perhaps the most important thing you can do to repair your credit from prison is to consistently make your payments on time. A huge factor in establishing your credit score is your payment history, so it is of the utmost importance that paying your bills on time is your first concern. To do this, you should set up a payment schedule to help you keep tabs on due dates. Another option is to have your agent on the streets sign you up for automated payments with your lender. Most lenders offer this option.

And here's another tip: Don't be afraid to contact your creditors directly. If you find yourself in a jam and aren't able to pay on time, many creditors are willing to temporarily make a more favorable payment plan for you just to help you through the rough patch. But to make this happen, it's up to you to reach out to them!

2.   Monitor Your Credit Reports: Whether you decide to get a passbook loan, a secured credit card, or get added to someone else's card as an approved user, you'll want to be sure to keep a close eye on your credit reports to confirm their accuracy and spot any possible errors. Even though you're incarcerated, you still have the right to access your credit report once a year for free. If you do come across any errors or inconsistencies, you'll want to address them as quickly as possible. To do this, gather whatever detailed documentation you have to support your grievance and enclose it with a letter to the credit bureaus. They are required by law to promptly investigate your claim and correct errors, as necessary.

   a.   Another smart thing you can do is think about enrolling in a credit monitoring service. They'll provide you with periodic updates and notify you of any changes or variations in your credit report.

3.   Your Credit Utilization: Your credit utilization is the amount of your available credit you're actually using. It's advised that you keep your credit utilization rate under 30% to preserve a good credit score. For instance, if your credit limit is

$1,000, you should only be using $300 at a time or less.

4. The Length of Your Credit History: This is the amount of time you've had open credit accounts. Usually, the longer your credit history, the better. This proves to lenders that you have a verifiable track record of dependably staying on top of your credit over time. This is another reason why it's important for you as an incarcerated person to start working to repair your credit now.

5. Making New Credit Applications: If you make too many credit applications over a brief window of time, it can negatively impact your credit score. When a bank or a potential lender pulls your credit report, it leaves evidence of something called a "hard inquiry." These can hurt your score temporarily, so it's not smart to apply for too many lines of credit at once.

a. All right, all you future millionaire prisoners, I've laid it all out for you in black and white. I know it might seem like a lot, and from where you're sitting, it's hard to bring yourself to take these first steps. Yet, if you're willing to apply yourself, it is 100% possible to repair your credit from prison. Will there be challenges? Of course. However, even to this day, whenever I'm faced with a challenge, I still remember the annoying advice of my parents: Nothing worth doing is ever easy, but that doesn't mean it can't be done!

PartTwo

INTRODUCTION

Very few people have sympathy for America's incarcerated population. And I get it! Growing up, I didn't either, but as I've gotten older, I've come to realize things are rarely so black and white. As humans, we are inherently flawed, and there is never a one size that fits all answer when it comes to imposing justice. Understandably, justice requires accountability on the part of the wrongdoer, and in today's society, that accountability is dispensed in the form of punishment. Whether that punishment comes in the form of fines, restitution, community service, probation, or incarceration, the intention seems to be ensuring that karma is maintained... what goes around comes around, right?

Yeah, that's all well and good, and sure, I agree with the basic principle of karma underlying justice.

Yet, there's something I do have a problem with...

Our government is so quick to dispense punishment whenever a citizen breaks one of their laws. Hell, they'll click those cuffs on you, arrest you, lock you up, and as if that's not bad enough, weigh you down with heavy fines without a second thought. Then, once you've been locked away, they'll nod approvingly and say, "justice has been served." To them, they are just maintaining the balance of karma in the world.

Now, what happens when it is them, the government that gets caught doing something wrong? What happens when it is the government that gets caught breaking one of their own rules? Do they then pursue justice with the same zeal they display when they're seeking to punish a regular Joe, like you and me? Because in a real democratic society, we invest great power in our government, and naturally, we expect the government we've empowered, to use their sense of discretion when exercising the power that we've trusted in them.

128

Unfortunately, however, that doesn't always happen, let me give you an example from my own experience.

In the beginning of 2022, after having been arrested for the long list of charges that I'm currently serving time for, my world was in shambles, and I was totally fucked. Having had my Camaro recently towed by the infamous PPA for having too many unpaid traffic tickets, and no money to pay the thousands of dollars I owed, being on day five of a meth binge, I came up with a brilliant idea to go to a car dealership and get a new car. As it is with anything you do while you're high on meth, however, nothing is ever as simple and easy as it sounds.

As I was walking out of the impound lot, having gathered all of my belongings from the Camaro, knowing that I'd never see it again, I formulated this plan. As I rode in the Uber to Cherry Hill I perfected my unknowingly idiotic plan, which at the time I had thought to be pure criminal mastermind genius, just as every plan you think up on meth is. Armed with a stolen driver's license and a COVID mask, I walked into a KIA dealership of all places, thinking that, due to COVID, I'd be able to test drive a car on my own. Just as I had when I bought the Camaro, a few months before, I asked to check out their nicest SUV.

The plan worked all the way up until it was time to go on the test drive. Where I had thought it would be as easy as filling out some quick paperwork, copying the stolen license of a guy who looked enough like me, get the keys, and take off, it became a whole lot more complicated when the salesman jumped in the car with me. I did the only thing that made sense at the moment. I took the car out for a test drive. Once we were far enough away I pulled over and looked right in the salesman's eyes and gave him a choice of either getting out or staying and coming over the bridge with me. Apparently, he didn't want to stay, because he jumped out of the car faster than I've ever seen in my life.

Surprisingly enough, especially how bad Jersey cops are, I made it over the Ben Franklin and back into Philly without incident. Even more surprisingly, I used the car in the commission of dozens of different crimes over the span of close to two weeks before getting into my first police chase in Kensington, which I had managed to get away from with little effort. You think after that, I'd get rid of the car and find a new one less actively hot on the police radar, but no, I continued driving it just as if it really was my own legitimate vehicle.

And it wasn't that I couldn't do it. Every time I pulled up in Kensington, I had people offering me good money for it, knowing it was hot. I should have sold it and stole another new car, being that it was so easy, but as crazy as it may sound, especially being a Kia, I fell in love with that car. I sound like an endorsement for Kia right now, but all I'm saying is that if you still think Kia is the same shitty cheap company they were ten years ago, go drive a Stinger GT or a Telluride. I had stolen the Sorento turbo, and that truck was nicer than most of the more expensive foreign cars all my friends drove. And for what it was, it was fast, not Trackhawk Jeep fast of course, but fast enough to get out on most normal cars, including cop cars.

As it always seems to be my luck, the very following day after getting into a police chase, even though it had lasted only minutes, I was around the Temple area of North Philly, stopped at a red light, music up, texting, and not paying attention. When of course, a cop car pulls up right next to me. Both cops were staring directly at me, no doubt they had immediately recognized the Kia, likely the most wanted stolen vehicle in the entire city.

As soon as I saw the police, I knew what it was. Not waiting for them to light me up or the chance to pull in front of me and box me in, I hit the gas and took off straight through the red light, barely missing a car. Having just gotten away from the police, believing in my driving skills and chances of getting away again, I took the police on one hell of a chase all through North Philly that certainly was one that went very viral, but not because of my amazing driving skills, more so, due to all of my epic failures, which of course, were all from being high out of my mind on meth.

In turn, as I was running, I believed I was a professional getaway driver in a Hollywood movie. Instead, that was all just in my mind which was sleep deprived and altered by drugs. In actual reality, I wasn't nearly doing as good a job driving as I thought I was. No, I stupidly drove right into a fenced parking lot, boxed myself in, and had to smash into a cop car to get out. I then hit a corner too sharp, messing up the front wheel to the point where the car wasn't drivable at all. So I ditched it and took off on foot.

Already deep in the shit at that point, and incapable of giving up in the type of mindset I was in, I ran up to the first car I saw that was waiting at a red light, forced the driver out, stole it, and desperately continued trying to escape from what it seemed like the entire Philadelphia Police Department.

I think it was at that point when I knew deep down that it was over for me, and I wasn't getting away this time. I stopped trying to get away so much as I started trying to just prolong the inevitable outcome, which was that I was heading back to prison. Deciding to enjoy the last little bit of freedom I had left, I connected my phone to the Lexus's Bluetooth, cranked up some of my favorite classic Flamerz Meek, chain smoked the rest of my pack of Camel Crush's, and as I sped through the back streets, I snorted whatever meth I had left on me, which was close to an Eight ball!

The chase continued up Broad Street into Olney before it finally ended abruptly when I ran a stop sign and crashed directly into the side of another car, totaling both vehicles. I was pretty badly banged up, more so from all the damn airbags than the actual crash. Who knew Lexus had so many freaking airbags? It felt like I was being punched from every direction.

You would have assumed that it was the end for me, but no! Ending it went right out the window the moment I finished off the remaining meth, and now I was zooted. My body was running off nothing except pure adrenaline and methamphetamine. Despite my injuries, I took off on foot running as fast as I could without having a clue where the hell I even was, or where I was going. I didn't make it very far before I managed to slip on black ice and fall right on my ass.

Unable at that time to feel any pain, for obvious reasons, I quickly jumped back to my feet, ready to run. The police, however, were already on me, so without even hesitating, I reacted by fighting what had felt like a horde of cops, all while the news chopper was above broadcasting everything. Obviously, you already know how it ends, as I am writing this from my cell in prison. The cops eventually prevailed over me and between the injuries from the crash, having been shot multiple times with Tasers, and getting the shit beat out of me, I woke up the following day in the hospital where I'd spend the next few days recovering from the ordeal before being transported to the county jail.

Needless to say, I had made what was already a bad situation into a much fucking worse ordeal, all because I was high and thought that I could get away. As I sat detoxing in county jail, the last thing I was concerned about was whether or not the judge had probably presided over the administration of my sentencing order for the court costs, fines, and restitution.

As far as I was concerned, I was caught up in the gears of a well-oiled judicial machine, a machine that simply never made mistakes. As I sat in jail reflecting on just how badly screwed I really was, I wasn't in the mindset to question the judicial system's diligence when it came to handling my paperwork. Like most people, I had just assumed that I was dealing with bureaucratic robots, experts at dotting their I's and crossing their T's, which kept people like me behind bars.

Eventually, I was convicted and sentenced to six years in prison. Once I got upstate and my friends and family began to send me money on my books (inmate trust account), I realized that the prison was taking 25% of all my incoming money for something called Act 84. Initially, I didn't think anything of it, because again, assuming that it was just part of Department of Correction policy, and there wasn't anything I could do about it. As time went on, however, it started adding up, and I started to notice the money that the prison was taking from me was becoming quite significant. This wasn't sitting quite right with me.

After speaking with other inmates who were having the same thing being done to them, I decided to go to the law library and learn more about what the hell Act 84 was, and why they were taking money for it. It turned out that I wasn't the only one who had been interested in it. As soon as I mentioned Act 84 to the law librarian, he knew exactly what I was talking about and had an entire folder specifically for it. Besides learning the reasons the DOC had the power to deduct money for court costs, fines, and restitution, there was an amazing amount of contradictory information. It didn't help either that

133

everyone who I talked to about it, of course in true jailhouse fashion, had completely different answers and explanations about it.

After weeks of reading up on the act and doing research, I still was no closer to finding an answer to stopping it. In fact, I had even more questions about it at that point than I did when I didn't know a thing about it when I first started my research. The only thing I learned was there were certain ways that I could possibly stop Act 84, and in theory, by doing so, stop the prison from deducting any more money from my account for the court costs and fines I owed. I did not have the ability, nor did I know enough about it to try to stop it on my own.

I needed a lawyer. The only problem was that I didn't have the money to hire a lawyer to help me file the right motions. I also did not have a great track record with having any success through the legal aid of jailhouse lawyers, so that wasn't an option for me either. Over the next several months, just as I had done back when I was in the county fighting my case, I searched for a pro bono attorney, legal aid group, or anyone who could help me with filing to stop Act 84 for free. You would think it's impossible, especially while you're incarcerated with such limited resources, but it's not. It's been my experience throughout my entire life, that very little is actually impossible. If you want something bad enough and are willing to put the work into getting it, more times than not, you will get it.

After hundreds of calls my family made on my behalf, after months of writing inquiry letters to hundreds of attorneys, firms legal groups, organizations, law projects, and many others, I finally found an attorney who was willing to take me on as a pro bono client and help me through the process of filing to stop Act 84.

If you are in the same situation as I was, in need of legal aid but can't afford it, I strongly suggest that your first step be to read my book "THE NATIONAL PRO BONO ATTORNEY DIRECTORY."

The lawyer started doing some digging, and sure enough, he found the loophole. After going through my case documents, it turned out my sentencing judge never put in the correct order authorizing the prison to take any money from my account for anything, including court costs and fines. Yet, as the DOC always does whatever they please, they took my money anyway. Amazingly, for the very first time in my life, the law actually worked for me rather than against me as it always had before. I was able to use it to my advantage to stop the prison from continuing to illegally take money from me under the guise of Act 84!

It had been a great sense of accomplishment for me. I, against all odds, not only found an attorney to take my case pro bono, but I fought the DOC, and I won! Afterward, though, as I talked to other inmates about my small feat against the prison taking my money, I quickly realized that very few of them actually knew what Act 84 was, let alone that it was possible to stop it and prevent the prison from taking any more of their money. Naturally, being the entrepreneur that I've always been, I saw the opportunity to make some money. I decided to create a legal guide for all of those incarcerated in Pennsylvania, in which I would lay out the steps and provide the necessary motions needed to successfully stop the prison from unlawfully deducting money from their inmate trust accounts for this Act.

I put together a booklet I had unimaginatively titled "THE PRISONER LEGAL GUIDE TO STOPPING THE PRISONS FROM TAKING YOUR MONEY." Although it was only for inmates in

Pennsylvania struggling with having their money being taken by Act 84, the unpublished booklet that, I had advertised in the Prison Legal News for only $10, sold like crazy. We couldn't make booklets fast enough. To my surprise, I started receiving letters and emails from inmates not only in Pennsylvania, but all across the country, thanking me for showing them how to protect their money from the prisons.

As expected, in true authoritarian fashion, the Pennsylvania Department of Corrections banned my legal guide all across the state. They claimed that the contents encouraged prisoners to circumvent legal obligations, specifically paying what they owed in court costs, fines, and restitution. This of course was complete bullshit. They were in the wrong by unlawfully taking money from inmates without a court order, and they did not want anyone learning how to stop them.

When I received the notification in the mail about my booklet being banned, I was torn. On one hand, I was kind of excited because my legal guide had obviously become so popular that the Department of Corrections felt compelled to keep it out of the hands of inmates in every single state prison. On the other hand, I was pissed. It wasn't like I had advised inmates to do anything illegal, or even against prison policies, and trust me I know them all very well. In fact, I actually had done the complete opposite. The guide I had written simply educated inmates on how to utilize the established legal channels to enforce the laws pertaining to Act 84 as well as their constitutional rights.

There had been nothing whatsoever wrong with what I had written. I simply exposed a way for inmates who had the same issue with the prison system as I had to exploit the same technicality that my lawyer used to successfully stop Act 84 and the deductions for me. In essence, I was giving everyone the loophole in the system. Clearly, the Department of Corrections hadn't liked that at all. They were doing everything in their power to keep inmates like you, from learning how to use the law to stop them from unlawfully taking your money. The shoe, it seems, was now on the other foot, and the powers that be were not happy.

All this brings me to the purpose of Part 2. In the following lessons, I will shine light on some important, but little known facts and statistics regarding the shocking truth of the American prison population. As you read through the information, be mindful of how much the prisons are getting away with, simply because too many inmates are not fully informed of what's really happening to them, their rights, or most importantly, what they can do to protect themselves from the prison. We all know why that is, it's no mystery that the prisons hold complete power over what they allow the inmates to have, and by doing so, they control what type of information reaches them.

Later in lesson 10, after opening your mind to these statistics, you'll find that I have included edited sample versions (so hopefully not to have this book banned as well) of the original motions my lawyer filed on my behalf to successfully stop the prison from taking any more of my money for as long as I'm incarcerated. Although these motions are specifically for Pennsylvania, I also included a generic sample motion that is comparable to other motions from other states, except it excludes Act 84. It basically cites stopping the prison from deducting money from your account for court costs and fines. The motion may help inmates in other states, depending upon your state and the details of your case.

Note:

I want to make something clear to everyone who reads this part of the book. In no way is this actually cancelling out whatever amount of money you may owe in court costs, fines, or restitution. I wish it would, however, if such a loophole exists, I've yet to find it. All this will do, if you are successful with your motion, is suspend the courts from being able to authorize the prison to deduct any money from you that you may owe for court costs and fines for the length of your incarceration, until you are released and can afford to resume making payments.

LESSON 7

2025 PRISON STATS AND FACTS FROM AN INDEPENDENT STUDY

What They Don't Want You to Know About

If the Department of Corrections is taking a percentage of money from your prison account for ACT-84 (PA only) or general court costs, fines, and restitution, they could very likely be doing so without the authority from the Courts and therefore doing so illegally. According to a 2025 national independent prison census study, there are around two million incarcerated inmates at any given time being housed in the 1,819 state correctional institutions across the United States. From that study, the following statistics are:

1.2M That is the estimated total number of state inmates in the U.S. who get a percentage deducted from their prison account by the DOC every time they receive money from family or friends, as well as their institutional pay earnings, to go towards their outstanding court costs, fines, and restitution that they owe.

720K That is the estimated total number of state inmates who are actually having their money taken illegally and without the necessary Court Order giving authorization to the Prison Inmate Accounting Office, and eligible to take legal action to stop the prison from deducting any more of their money without authorization.

68% That is the estimated percent of the above 720,000 state inmates who believe that the deductions being made to their prison account are completely legitimate and just part of normal DOC policy, but have no idea that in fact those deductions are being made illegally and can be easily stopped by filing the right legal motions, Motions just like the ones that are included in this book.

23% That is the estimated percent of state inmates who know that their rights are being violated by the DOC illegally deducting a percentage of all their money but still taking no legal action toward trying to stop it.

9% That is the estimated very few inmates out of the staggering 720,000 who know that their rights are being violated by the DOC and actually do something about it and take legal action to stop the DOC from illegally deducting a percentage of all of their incoming money without the Court's authorization.

$800 That is the national average rate an attorney charges to create and file one legal motion. Of course, that rate can easily be higher depending on where you live, and the local rates being charged. Up until now, hiring an attorney was the only realistic and reliable way, other than using a jailhouse lawyer for state inmates to be able to file the right legal motion to fight against the DOC and have any chance at succeeding at stopping the illegal deductions of money being made to their prison account. But not anymore! Now you can save hundreds of dollars in legal fees and weeks if not possibly months of back and forth communication by filing the right motion yourself with the included, professionally drafted, sample Legal Motion.

LESSON 8

UNDERSTANDING THE LAW AND YOUR PRISONER RIGHTS

The Facts That You Need to Know

- The Department of Corrections does not have the legal authority to deduct any amount of money or a percentage of money from a state inmate's prison account for noninternal institutional purposes including court costs, fines, and restitution without a written Court Order from the trial or sentencing judge imposing such specific deductions be made to the inmate's prison account by the prison's Inmate Accounting Office.

- In order for a Court Order to be lawfully issued by the Court giving the DOC the necessary authority to be able to deduct any amount or percentage of money from a state inmate's prison account, a hearing determining the inmate's financial ability to pay the imposed court costs, fines, and restitution must be held.

- If the trial or sentencing Judge did not specify inside your Judgment of Sentence or Sentencing Order that the method of payment which your imposed court costs, fines, and restitution must be paid and the DOC id deducting any percentage from out of the money that you receive from family or friends, and from your institutional earnings, the DOC is in fact making those deductions unlawfully due to the fact that there is no existing Court Order giving the prison's Inmate Accounting Office the authority to take any amount of money from you for such purposes.

Are you Eligible to Stop Your Money From Being Taken Illegally?

YES! If your case meets the following qualifying requirements stated in this lesson.

Too many state inmates all across the country are being affected by the Department of Corrections violating their rights by illegally deducting a percentage (25% in PA) of all the money that they receive from family, friends, and Institutional earnings through work, programs, and schooling. And the worst part is that the DOC and all of the institutions are getting away with it because most state inmates have no idea that these deductions to their money are actually in fact being made in many cases completely illegally due to not having the needed authorization of a valid Court Order.

Therefore, hundreds of thousands of state inmates who believe that the deductions are perfectly legitimate and cannot be stopped have no choice but to accept the deductions being made to their prison account. When in fact, for many of those state inmates, that isn't the case at all, and the deductions can very much and easily be stopped by taking legal action against the DOC. If you are one of the many state inmates who meet the following qualifying requirements listed below, then you very well may be eligible to put a stop to your institution taking any more of your money indefinitely with the motions that are included in this course.

The following are the most important qualifying requirements in order to be eligible to take legal action and file Legal Motions against the DOC to stop the illegal deductions of your money in most states.

- Your Judgment of Sentence does not specify the method of payment and does not give specific Court-ordered authorization to the Department of Corrections or the Prison Inmate Accounting Office to be able to Lawfully deduct any percent of money from your prison account for ACT-84 or general court costs, fines, and restitution that you owe.

- You did not have an official Court hearing on your financial ability to pay the imposed court costs, fines, and restitution that you owe.

- You did not have a pre-sentence investigation, or you did, and the investigation was unable to provide a basis regarding your ability to pay court costs, fines, and restitution, and therefore, it did not support the Court Order stating that you have to pay them while incarcerated.

- If your prison's Inmate Accounting Office has at any time during your incarceration or is currently deducting any percentage of money from your institutional earnings and all other incoming funds that you receive from family or friends to go towards your owed court costs, fines, and restitution.

- You currently earn a total amount of $500 or less per month for tax-deductible employment. NOTE: Prison earnings, including your work pay, is not legally considered tax-deductible income.

LESSON 9

Guide to Properly Filling out and Filing Motions

All of the required information can usually be found in your original Judgement of Sentence and/or new commit paperwork, i.e., Inmate Status Sheet. If you do not have the needed information, you can write to your County Clerk of Courts for a copy of your Judgement of Sentence or request a copy of your Inmate Status Sheet/sentencing information from your institution's Record Office, and information on all your court costs, fines, and/or restitution owed from the Inmate Accounting/Business Office.

Unfortunately, due to many state's Institutional mail restrictions and strict policies prisoners are unable to receive such Motion forms through the mail. Many books similar to mine, dedicated to providing prisoners across the country with the important information that they need to know, but the Department of Corrections doesn't want them to know are being banned and not let into the institutions under the rule that such motions are designed to help inmates circumvent their legal and financial obligations to the courts - which is not the case with my Motions and furthermore even if that was the case it is a legal Motion to be filed with the County Court and has nothing to do with the DOC and therefore should not be intercepted and denied by the institution.

Because of this, I am unable to include completed fill-in-the-blank Motion forms for you to simply fill out and file as I had originally planned to do. Now I have to write the Motion forms out in a certain way that will not be so obvious to those who are tasked with inspecting new publications and determining whether or not to allow them in. I have tried to make it as easy as possible for you to read and understand without bringing any unwanted attention to the Motion forms.

It is important that you do not try to fill out the included sample motions and send them out to be filed. Furthermore, it is important for you to make certain when filling out the respected motion that all of the information you put down is, to the best of your knowledge, accurate and true.

Sample Motion Instructions

Followed the guidelines to recreate each of the three sample motion forms. In the following lesson. Below are the official titles of the motions to use instead of the sample motion titles currently on the motions.

- Sample motion form (A) title is" MOTION TO STOP DEDUCTIONS OF COURT COSTS, FINES, AND RESTITUTION."

- Sample motion form (B) title is" MOTION TO STOP ACT 84 DEDUCTIONS."

- Sample motion form (C) title is" MOTION FOR ACT 84 REIMBURSEMENT."

If you're in an institute that allows you to receive these kinds of Motion forms then you can have your people go to my website and print out the Motion forms for free and mail it to you so that you can fill it out and file it. Otherwise, you will have to use these sample motions as a template to retype/rewrite the Motion forms yourself, complete them, and then file them.

Guidelines After Completing The Motion

Once you have completed filling out the Legal Motion form, you will need to make copies for all interested parties involved. Typically, you will need to send it out to four separate people. The four people that you need to send a copy to are:

- The Count Clerk of Courts
- The County District Attorney's Office
- The attorney that is assigned to your case
- The judge

Make sure you keep a copy of the completed Legal Motion for your personal records.

Note: You can obtain the necessary addresses for all of the above parties either online or in your prison law library.

Including Necessary Documents

Along with the completed Legal Motion, you will need to include additional documents of proof, otherwise known as exhibits. For both motions (A) and (B) you will need to include the Following two exhibits:

Make a copy of your **Order of Judgment-of Sentence**, and/or **Sentencing Order**. This is the official court document from the sentencing Judge that orders the specific details for court costs, fines, and restitution. Remember to put the title EXHIBIT "A" on the top of every page.

Make a copy of All your Institutional monthly account statements. Highlight all of the Act-84 deductions that had been made to your money. Remember to put the tittle EXHIBIT "B" on the top of every page.

LESSON 10

Letter to The Judge

DATE: _____

NAME: _____

DOC#: _____

DOCKET NUMBERS(S):

_____

_____

To The Honorable

_____

My name is _____, and I
am currently incarcerated in _____
state Correctional Institute. I have been incarcerated since
_____. I am respectfully Requesting a time-
served sentence on my court costs, fines, and restitution owed
on the above docket(s). My anticipated release date is

_____.

If your Honor is not inclined to Sentence me to time served for
my court costs, Fines, and restitution owed, I am respectfully
requesting that I be allowed .

IN THE HONORABLE COURT OF

_____, **County**

_____

_____	:
Plaintiff	:
	:
Vs	: Case no:_____
	:
_____	:
Defendant	

SAMPLE MOTION (A)

1. Plaintiff was sentenced on_____ to a term of _____ to (_____months_____years), and was ordered to pay court costs, fines, and/or restitution of $_____.

2. Plaintiff avers that the Inmate Accounting Office at _____, has been deducting _____ From his/her inmate trust account every time the Plaintiff receives nominal "gifts" of money from Family and Friends, as well as his/her institutional earnings, which is $_____ per month.

3. The Department of corrections lacks the authority to deduct court costs, fines, and/or restitution from an

inmate's trust account without the presence of a written COURT ORDER IMPOSING such Deductions.

4. Plaintiff was never given the opportunity for pay court costs, fines, and/or restitution.

5. Plaintiff is unable to make payments at this time due to his/her continued incarceration and if motion is to be granted he/she will contact the court immediately upon his/her release, to set up meaningful payment arrangements for his/her court costs, fines, and/or restitution.

6. Plaintiff Avers pursuant to the attached signed COURT ORDER " Exhibit A" by the Trial/ Sentencing Judge, Showing an absence within his/her written and signed COURT ORDER mandating the deduction of any monies from the Plaintiff's inmate trust account, institutional pay and from all nominal "gifts" of money received from his/her family and Friends, for the payment of court costs, fines, and/or restitution. THEREFORE the deductions made, were in fact illegal and unlawful, and the plaintiff respectfully requests that this honorable court, set forth an ORDER, directly the Inmate Accounting office at_____ to CEASE and DESIST the deductions being made for court costs, fines, and/or restitution.

   a. Please refer to attached EXHIBIT "A" judgement of sentence/ court order.
   b. And attached EXHIBIT "B" inmate's institutional account statement's for Further proof of the illegal and unlawful deductions.

7. The interest of Justice will be served If this motion is granted, and the Honorable Court will not be prejudiced.

WHEREFORE, the Plaintiff prays and humbly requests that this Honorable Court GRANT his/her court costs, fines, and has the ability to make payments upon obtaining gainful employment.

Respectfully Submitted,

Date: _____

DOC#: _____

NAME: _____

IN THE COURT OF COMMON PLEAS

OF_____, COUNTY

PENNSYLVANIA

CRIMINAL DIVISION

_____ :	
Plaintiff :	
Vs :	Case No:_____
:	
COMMONWEALTH OF :	
PENNSYLVANIA	

SAMPLE MOTION FORM (B)

AND NOW comes,_____, Plaintiff proceeding in Pro Se capacity, herby moves the Honorable Court for an **ORDER** to **STOP** the unlawful deductions of money being made to the Plaintiffs inmate trust account for court costs, fines, and restitution. In support thereof, the Plaintiff avers the following reasons and facts set forth below:

1. Plaintiff was sentenced on_____ to a term of _____to (_____months_____years), and was ordered to pay court costs, fines, and/or restitution of $_____.

2. Plaintiff avers that the Inmate Accounting Office at S.C.I._____, has been deducting 25% from his/her

inmate trust account every time the Plaintiff receives nominal "gifts" of money from family and friends, as well as his/her institutional earnings, which is $_____ per month.

3. The Department of Corrections lacks the authority to deduct court costs, fines, and restitution from an inmate's trust account in the absence of a written COURT ORDER imposing such deductions.

4. Plaintiff was not given a hearing on his/her financial ability to pay court costs, fines, and restitution.

5. S. _____ Defendant is unable to make payments at this time due to his/her continued incarceration and will contact the Court immediately upon his/her release, to set up meaningful payment arrangements for his/her court costs, fines, and restitution.

6. Plaintiff avers pursuant to the attached signed COURT ORDER by the Plaintiff's Trial/Sentencing Judge, showing an absence within his/her written and signed COURT ORDER mandating the deduction of 25% from Plaintiff's inmate trust account, institutional pay and from all monies received as a "GIFT" from family and friends, for the deductions of court costs, fines, and restitution pursuant to ACT 84. The deductions made, were illegal and unlawful, and Plaintiff requests this Honorable Court, set forth an ORDER, directing the Inmate Accounting Office at S.C.I to CEASE and DESIST the 25% deductions for court costs, fines, and restitutions.

   a. Please refer to attached EXHIBIT "A" Judgement of Sentence/Court Order.

   b. And attached EXHIBIT "B" inmate's Institutional account statement for further proof of the illegal and unlawful 25% deductions.

159

7.   The interest of justice will be served if this Motion is granted, and the Commonwealth will not be prejudiced.

WHEREFORE, the Plaintiff prays and humbly requests that this Honorable Court GRANT his/her Motion and issue an ORDER to the Inmate Accounting Office at S.C.I_____ to immediately suspend ACT 84 deductions of his/her court costs, fines, and restitution until he/she is released and has the ability to make payments upon obtaining gainful employment.

                              Respectfully Submitted,

                              Date:_____

                              DOC#_____

                              Name:_____

                              DOC#_____

160

IN THE COURT OF COMMON PLEAS OF

_____PENNSYLVANIA COUNTY

COMMONWEALTH OF PENNSYLVANIA

vs.

CASE No:_____

Defendant

SAMPLE MOTION C

AND NOW COMES,_____Defendant proceeding in Pro Se capacity, herby moves the Honorable Court to GRANT Defendant's Motion for ACT 84 Reimbursement. In support thereof, the Defendant avers the following:

1. Plaintiff avers that the Inmate Accounting Office at S.C.I _____ has been deducting 25% from his inmate trust account every time Defendant receives nominal "GIFTS" of money from family, and friend's, as well as his institutional pay. This action is illegal and unlawful pursuant to an abuse of a valid COURT ORDER signed by the Defendant's Trial/Sentencing Judge. See COMMONWEALTH V. LEBAR, 860 A.2d 1105 (PA. Super. 2017); see also COMMONWEALTH V. SPOTZ, 972 A.2d 125 (PA. 2009).

2. Plaintiff avers SPOTZ went on to state that, in BOYD V. D.O.C., 831 A.2d 779 (2003),

ACT 84 does not apply where an inmate's "asserts" no such ORDER has been made by the Sentencing Court. Id., 130-131.

3. Plaintiff avers that the deductions of 25% pursuant to ACT 84 is an illegal and incorrect deduction, due to the fact, said deduction's, occurred in the absence of a valid COURT ORDER of record issued by the Trial/Sentencing Judge. The deduction of 25% shall not occur based on the word of the Clerk of Court's, saying ACT 84 applies to a Plaintiff's case.

4. The Department of Corrections lacks the authority to deduct court costs, fines, and restitution from an inmate's trust account in the absence of a written COURT ORDER imposing such deductions.

5. Plaintiff avers even though there was an oral pronouncement for costs made in the sentencing notes, but the sentencing Court failed to reduce the same to written form and include the same in the Judgement of Sentence signed by the Trial/Sentencing Judge, the oral pronouncement is therefore NULL and VOID. See COMMONWEALTH V. QUINIAN, 639 a.2D 1235, 1239 (PA Super 1992).

6. Plaintiff avers pursuant to COMMONWEALTH V. EVANS, 385 A.2d 540 (PA. Super.

1975). The "only" sentence recognized by the PA Appellate Court's is a "written"

Judgement of Sentence "signed" by the Trial/Sentencing Judge.

Plaintiff avers pursuant to the attached signed COURT ORDER by the defendant's Trial/Sentencing Judge, showing an absence within his/her written and signed COURT ORDER mandating the deduction of 25% from Defendant's inmate trust account, institutional pay and from all monies received as a "GIFT" from family and friends, for the deductions of court costs, fines, and restitution pursuant to ACT 84. The deductions made were illegal and unlawful, and the Defendant requests this Honorable Court, set forth an ORDER, directing the Inmate Accounting Office at S.C.I to REFUND all monies illegally deducted from his/her inmate account, as a result of ACT 84 deductions of 25% of nominal gifts and Institutional pay.

Please refer to attached EXHIBIT "A" Judgement of Sentence/Court Order.

And attached EXHIBIT "B" inmate's Institutional account statement for further proof of the illegal and unlawful 25% deductions.

7. The interest of justice will be served if this Motion is granted, and the Commonwealth will not be prejudiced.

WHEREFORE, the Plaintiff prays and humbly requests that this Honorable Court GRANT his/her Motion and issue an ORDER to the Inmate Accounting Office at S.C.I ---   ...   to immediately suspend ACT 84 deductions and reimburse and apply to Defendant's inmate account all monies deducted from his/her inmate trust account (SEE EXHIBIT "B") pursuant to ACT 84.

Respectfully Submitted,

Date:_____

Name:_____

DOC#_____

DATE:_____

NAME:_____

DOC#_____ DOB:_____

DOCKET   NUMBER(S):   _____
_____
_____

To The Honorable

My name is _____ and I am currently incarcerated in State Prison. I have been incarcerated since _____. I am respectfully requesting a time-served sentence on my court costs, fines, and restitution owed on the above docket(s). My anticipated release date is _____

If your Honor is not inclined to sentence me to time served for my court costs, fines, and restitution owed, I am respectfully requesting that I be allowed to set up a new payment plan to begin upon my release from custody. For the reason that I am not able to pay financially at the present time.

Please let me know, at your earliest convenience, if your Honor is willing to grant my request. Thank you for your time and consideration in this matter.

Respectfully submitted,

NAME:_____

DOC#:_____

RETURN MAILING ADDRESS:

_____

_____

_____

Secrets to Finding a Pro Bono Attorney

Introduction to Pro Bono Attorneys

Lawyers are expensive. You know that already. In fact, the financial costs of having good legal representation are often so high that the average person can't even afford an attorney. But what does that mean for the average guy in prison? Are we screwed?

Does that mean "justice" is available only to the wealthiest members of society? Unfortunately, it often seems like it, but it isn't supposed to be that way. After all, according to the U.S. Judicial System, access to legal counsel is a basic human right - and a founding principle when it comes to fairness before the law. Yet, far too often, the rights of the common man get trampled beneath the feet of those with deeper pockets simply because your average Joe doesn't have the financial resources to afford adequate legal representation.

That's why pro bono lawyers play a crucial role. By offering their legal services free of charge, some attorneys give the poor a pinprick of light at the end of the tunnel.

The Difference Between Pro Bono and Legal Aid

"Pro Bono" is a Latin phrase translating to "for the public good." And, in the legal profession, the phrase pertains to work a lawyer does at no cost to their client.

Similarly, a "legal aid" office is a group of lawyers who represent clients who can't afford to pay for legal services. The difference is this: Legal Aid groups are generally composed of full-time professionals who deal exclusively with the poor, whereas pro bono attorneys work mostly with fee-paying clients but will occasionally take on a case for free.

A common mistake amongst people seeking counsel free of cost is to assume that a pro bono attorney is preferable than counsel offered by legal aid groups. While this might sometimes be true, it's more often the case that legal aid groups are more well-versed in the areas of the law that poor people most commonly seek assistance with (i.e., matters pertaining to welfare, housing, and consumer law). So don't presume that, if a non-legal aid attorney takes your case for free, you're assured a better outcome. Legal Aid groups are usually more experienced at handling the cases of poor and incarcerated clients.

That being said, most legal aid organizations tend to only take on civil cases, not criminal. This is because criminal defendants who can't pay for an attorney get court- appointed counsel (a public defender). So, if you're looking to appeal a current criminal case, a better option would be to seek a pro bono attorney, especially if you have a good legal issue. Because, while legal aid groups are often looking to effect broad legal reform, pro bono attorneys tend to look for winnable individual cases that might polish their reputations. For instance, a hotshot criminal defense attorney might take on your case if he thinks he can overturn it - obviously, it would be good for him because he'd get to show off what a great lawyer he is to potential paying clients (while also getting to look like "a man of the people").

Of course, though we all would like pro bono attorneys to be a dime a dozen, the reality is that they aren't. States don't require pro bono work as essential to maintaining a law license. But the American Bar Association does encourage all attorneys to dedicate at least 50 hours a year to volunteer legal counsel for those who otherwise couldn't afford legal representation

Tips on Where to Start Your Pro Bono Search

If you feel you need pro bono counsel, see if you can have your agent or a loved one on the street look into your local or state bar association. If they visit the association's website, they may come across attorneys willing to take on select cases for free or they could always reach out to the state bar association directly.

Another option is to scout around a local law school or its website. Some law schools allow students under the supervision of qualified attorneys to take cases free of charge.

Also, the American Bar Association has a great website full of resources. They even allow some visitors to ask questions to pro bono attorneys.

Finally, if you are in the military, are a veteran, or have a military family member, there is a great list of links and resources on the Military Pro Bono Project website.

Frankly, with the Internet these days, there is a massive amount of information available online to anyone in need of free or low-cost legal counsel. With a little effort, your friends or loved ones on the street should have no problem connecting with the resources you need. Just remember, be persistent and be patient - the legal system moves at a glacial pace. Whatever you want to achieve won't happen overnight, but it is possible to secure good legal counsel at no cost to you.

You just have to know where to look.

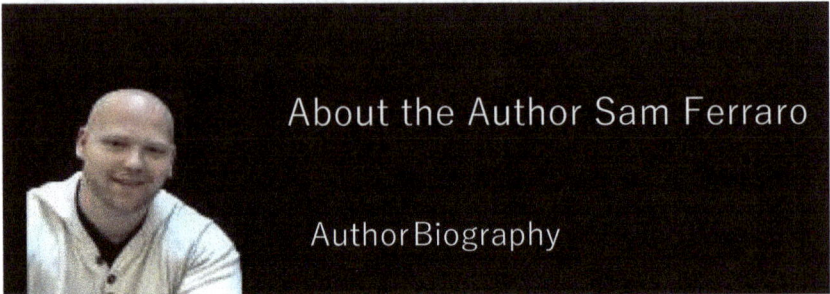

About the Author Sam Ferraro

Author Biography

Sam Ferraro is the founder of the publishing company, The Prisoner Press, and author of the popular book series – The Shit Prisoners Need To Know. An educational self-help series created for both incarcerated individuals and ex-offenders. His books are based on his own real life experience, hard learnt lessons, and knowledge from living on both sides of the prison walls.

His books, however, do not only benefit those who are incarcerated or out on parole. But everyone who seeks to discover success in the most challenging of circumstances and unlikeliest of places. Having spent nearly a decade behind bars altogether since his first incarceration in 2012, and even longer as an addict and criminal living the fast lifestyle in Philadelphia, Sam today is well regarded as an expert on all the subjects pertaining to the physical, mental, and emotional afflictions that are associated with being incarcerated, long term institutionalization, addiction, and of the criminal minded.

Unfortunately, it is that same unorthodox criminal lifestyle that Sam has chosen to live for most of his life that has made him the expert he is today, that subsequently has caused society to write him off, labeling him as a dangerous and untrustworthy criminal. In today's woke landscape, this is typical of how our society defines and unjustly judges all prisoners and ex-offenders. As a general stereotype instead of how they should, as an individual human being who has made mistakes in their lives — just as everyone has.

The truth of it is, just as it is with most others who are like him, Sam is so much more than just a felon, drug addict, or prison number. Everything that he has been able to overcome and accomplish, all while being incarcerated, is the perfect testament of how much more there is to him than what society would like for you to believe.

To better understand the fundamental purpose of the series Sam's created, you first need to understand who Sam is and, more importantly, who he used to be. What follows is a brief account of Sam's life, in his own words:

"Well, I guess I'll start from the beginning. I was born in Largo, Florida, where I was adopted by a well-off family as soon as I came into the world. Initially, I was raised in Bellair, an upper-class neighborhood, that was within walking distance from the beach, country club golf course, and the famous Biltmore Hotel. I lived there until I was eight years old when, in what felt like overnight, my life drastically changed — my parents got a divorce. Looking back, I realize it's something a lot of kids go through, but at the time, it felt like my world had been flipped upside-down. For the next several years, it was two Christmases, two birthdays, etcetera. You know the deal.

"By the time I turned 12 years old, neither of my parents were able to handle me anymore. I'd become so bad that they decided to send me away to a boarding school in Delaware. It was called Cedars Academy in the small town of Bridgeville. Man, I hated that place. It was no more than a year before I got kicked out. At that point, I thought I'd be going back down to Florida, but it turned out my mom had moved up to Philly to be closer to me.

"I went to a charter school in Center City, Philadelphia, until I was about 16 when I got kicked out of there, too, after I got into some trouble. The price again, I was sent packing to another boarding school – this was a place called the Patterson School in North Carolina. Can you guess what happened there? Yep, I got kicked out. This time, instead of going home, I was shipped straight away across the country to a Dr. Phil-sponsored troubled teen program in Utah called the Turnabout Ranch. Honestly, if I'd known that's where I was going to end up, I would've behaved when I was going to school in Philly.

"Anyway, once I got the hell out of Dr. Phil's place, I finally landed at my last boarding school in Idaho, the North Woods Academy. And that's how, at long last, I graduated from high school. Then it was back to Philly to live with my mom."

Sam's adult criminal record began shortly thereafter when, at the age of just 18, he got his first simple drug possession charge. "I was in the car with my friend and two girls coming back from a party near Temple University. It was probably close to 5:00 in the morning and, of course, with our luck, we got pulled over.

My boy was on probation already for a drug charge and had whatever was left of the weed we'd been smoking on him. Not wanting to get jammed up again, he tried getting one of the girls to take and hide it, but neither one of them would do it. At the time, besides a couple arrests that never went anywhere, I didn't have a record. Not wanting to see my friend go back to jail, I decided to grab the weed and take the charge.

Sam was arrested and would be sentenced to probation. After getting released from the district later on that day, he was picked up by his boy who he had taken the charge for. Obviously grateful for what Sam had done for him he decided to show his appreciation by putting him on, a small gesture that to him seemed like he was doing his friend a favor at the time, but what had been in reality the very pivoting point of Sam's life where he began his decent down the wrong path in which there would be no coming back from.

"Before this point in my life the only drug, besides trying ecstasy a few times, I had ever really used was marijuana, but that quickly changed. In the first couple weeks of me selling weed and hanging out with my boy and his crew I'd end up trying just about every type of street drug imaginable. Some drugs I liked better than others, and some not at all. It wasn't until I tried cocaine for the very first time I knew that was it. I had found my drug.

Of course, I was young and had no way of seeing it for what it really was at the time, because it all was so new and exciting for me. But my life and the trajectory of my future would change forever in that very moment I did my first line. After that, I started using coke more and more regularly until it became a daily habit for me. As my addiction – although I didn't consider it a problem, let alone an addiction back then – progressed so did my hustle, I went from selling weed, a relatively low level and harmless hustle, to selling coke, a much more lucrative and dangerous hustle. And because money was no object at the time I discovered that I was in a unique position where I could afford to buy weight from my boy for a discounted price.

Package it up myself and then sell whatever I didn't use to my customers, friends, and at college parties to make even more money.

Sam continued dealing until later that same year he was arrested on more serious charges that involved operating a business without a license and unlawful sale of alcohol. Many of Sam's friends and customers were students from local colleges – even though he wasn't a student himself – and with all the limitations on where one could go to party in the city being under 21, Sam saw an opportunity to capitalize on that he took full advantage of.

Using every bit of money he had saved up, Sam created his own spot, outside the reach of all the city regulations and the law, where his friends and anyone else could come hangout, use, drink, and party. He rented a large office space right outside the expensive prime real estate of downtown, but still within a quick cab ride from all the hot spots in the city and the colleges.

Knowing exactly what guys his age wanted, Sam hired college girls to dance and bartend, a DJ, and his crew to provide the drugs and when needed security. It was just the right thing at the perfect time, and Sam's idea paid off big for him. The spot quickly became the unofficial hangout for students and young professionals alike.

Word of Sam's spot went viral and spread across the city and every nearby college campus. Within a matter of weeks the place, which had no official name and was commonly known as simply the spot, reached heights of popularity and success that neither Sam nor his friends had ever thought possible. So much so that the spot was packed every day as a place to come, hangout, even purchase and use drugs. And full, with a line of people waiting to get in to party almost nightly, bringing in even more money now that he had an established and permanent location for him and his crew to deal out of. And, of course, the secret to the success of the spot, having no regulations or law to adhere too, there essentially were no rules, just about any and everything went inside the place. Something no other legitimate bar or club could offer.

Unfortunately, it was this same popularity that made the spot such a hit — and Sam more money than he knew what to do with — which also eventually landed it on the radar of the Philadelphia Police Department vice squad. After his spot was raided and Sam, along with several of his friends who were part of his crew were arrested, he spent a couple months in county jail — Sam's very first time in jail. Having no other choice, Sam had no access to his money, which was mostly all cash, to post bail and his parents unwilling to help him out of the mess he'd made for himself.

While in jail awaiting his court date, Sam would learn of an entirely new money making scheme that would enable him to make just as much money, if not even more, faster and without any of the risks of dealing drugs. Of course, he was once again all in on what he believed to be the perfect opportunity. And he came out of jail excited and fully committed to pursuing this new plan.

Sam was now at the fateful point of no return. The unfortunate narrative of his future set, walking out of jail Sam no longer was a normal teenager who only pushed boundaries slightly and skated around the law sometimes. He now was a full blown criminal who lived outside society and its laws altogether. As it is the case for so many in Sam's situation, they are blind to reason and reality, unable to see where they are headed. For Sam, it didn't help that the group of misfits he called friends were all hardheaded young criminals — very much like himself — who made committing crime and living the fast lifestyle seem normal, even cool and thrilling. But in fact reality was something completely different, a hard lesson Sam consequentially wouldn't learn for a long time.

Once released from jail, having been sentenced to county probation being that his friends never told the police he was behind it all and only being charged with misdemeanors due to his name being on the office lease, Sam immediately went to work Putting his newly discovered scheme into action. Having learnt from his mistakes with his last venture, Sam went into it with an entirely new mindset. This time he would keep it under the radar and unlike before he would do it all by himself without anyone knowing what he was up to.

The scheme was a straightforward in and out rental scam. Sam would locate houses for sale in the nicer areas of South Philly – where he also lived – that were unoccupied and had been on the market for a while. He then would schedule a showing to get more information from the listing agent and case the house to determine whether or not it was the right fit.

If it was, he would use the rest of the time he was in the house to plan out how he would break into it. From what intel he got from the agent, Sam would use it to figure the best time to use the house for the scam. After breaking into the house – typically it was as simple as leaving a window or side door unlocked while at the showing – Sam would change the lock on the front door so he had his own keys to come and go anytime he pleased without raising any suspicion with the other neighbors, switch the existing "for sale" sign with his own "for rent" sign, and using the photos from off the relator's website post his own advertisements online and on social media.

Once he received enough interest from potential renters,

Sam would start showing the house to as many individuals as he could, privately over the course of a week or so. He then would go through the process of renting out the house to each and every unexpecting renter who wanted the house. Of course, he wasn't actually renting the house to any of them, he only was making it seem as if he was. But, with Sam being a young, sharp dressing, clean-cut, good looking guy who could be very personable, to all of the renters the entire set-up appeared completely legitimate.

As he was with all his criminal ventures starting off, Sam had been very successful with his newest scheme. Mostly due to the fact that he was very convincing, Sam undeniably had natural Skills of a master manipulator. He drafted up custom leases that he would have the renters sign, schedule a move-in date, and after taking a cash payment of typically a couple thousands of dollars for first and last month rent, and a security deposit, Sam would hand over a copy of the front door key.

It wouldn't be until weeks later, when all those who thought they had rented the house arrived to finally move in, that they would discover that they weren't the only ones there trying to move into the same house. Only then did they learn that they had fallen victim to Sam's scam. And just as he had planned it, the victims knowing virtually nothing of his true identity beyond what he looked like, there was nothing that the police could do besides file a report a report which would never be pursued by a detective.

Sam went on to perfect the scam, making tens of thousands of dollars every couple weeks like clockwork, without ever coming close to being caught. Many would argue that with the kind of money he had made from his scheme, which reached well into the six figures by the first few months,

Sam could have and should have stopped while he was ahead and walked away from being a criminal, using the money to set himself for a comfortable and legitimate life. But it always seems so obviously simple to all those on the outside looking in. Yet, for those actually living it, it's never that obvious or ever that simple.

The truth is, Sam didn't have hundreds of thousands of dollars squirreled away under his mattress. He spent just as much as he made. Walking away wasn't an option for him. Between his expensive drug habit and having developed an insatiable appetite for the finer things in life, he would often end up broke before he even started on his next scam, regardless of whether he made $5,000 or $50,000. Sam was caught in the perpetual never ending loop of the fast lifestyle, the same life he had become addicted too.

As far as Sam was concerned, it was easy come, easy go. A common mindset for those living that type of fast money lifestyle. And Sam was no exception. His greed, coupled with his mentality of indifference and invincibility fueled his ambition to continue pushing the boundaries of what he could do and get away with. The more he got away with the further he pushed. Completely ignorant to the dangers he was all out sprinting towards, dangers he was unable to see because his actions were normal in the life he lived, and the circles he moved in.

Sam would continue to recklessly pursue his illegal schemes and push the limits for almost an entire year, until inevitably it all came to an end. Sam's ultimate downfall was his own doing. Having successfully broken into and used dozens of property's all over the city to scam hundreds of thousands of dollars without ever coming remotely close to being caught, he felt untouchable, convinced he could do whatever he wanted without any consequences, and because of that Sam pushed his limits too far. After learning that he was being evicted from his own South Philly house, he unwisely decided to use the house for his next scam – a scam which the local news would later dub the "South Philly Rental Scam."

And that's exactly what he did, scamming several unexpecting renters before having to move out. In fact, Sam scheduled their move in dates for the very next day after he himself moved out. A week later, after police learned of his true identity from his previous landlord, Sam was set-up and arrested. His good luck, seemingly, had run out. Although, it wouldn't appear that his luck ran out completely, as he never was charged in connection with any of the more than twenty property's he had broken into and used to scam more than a hundred people.

Sam was convicted on several counts of theft by deception for fraudulently renting out a property he didn't own. Through a plea deal made by his attorney the charges were all lowered to misdemeanors and Sam received five more years of probation. A deal he was all too happy to take, as it would allow him to avoid jail time. But accepting that much time under probation supervision would later prove to be a deal that Sam strongly regretted ever making.

Now, having got a taste of what it's like to live on the other side of both the law and society – and having received little more than a slap on the wrist each of the times he had been arrested – Sam was all in on living the fast criminal lifestyle at that point. For him, he couldn't imagine living his life any other way. For the next couple years, while still on probation, Sam cannily evaded authorities as he continued his criminal ventures. Each crime he committed was more bold than the last until, he was regularly committing serious felony offenses that, if caught, carried with them lengthy prison sentences.

Sam went back to selling drugs, but it was no longer enough for him, it had lost its cool and exciting facade. He jumped from one criminal scheme to the next, committing a wide range of crimes for almost a year, until discovering an entirely new and intriguing way to make money and establish himself as a player in the criminal world. Ever since his very first venture with the spot he created, he knew he was an entrepreneur and longed to have his own criminal enterprise to run.

"No matter what I tried doing, I always would end up back dealing, that was my fall back plan for everything. And as hard as I looked I couldn't find my own thing, it was always just other people's hustles that I piggy backed off of. I was done with it all, and that's when I got the opportunity to help one of my boys start an escort service. Yeah, it wasn't mine and I'd just be part of someone else's venture, again, but it got me out of the hood, which was at least a good start.

Sam started driving for the escort service, but would continue selling drugs, only now instead of having to sell on the block, he sold to both the girls who he drove and their clients that they provided services too. It wasn't long until Sam realized that he had finally found what he wanted his thing to be.

"I had the best of both worlds. I was making money driving the girls, which if I'm being honest really wasn't a job at all, I was making money selling the girls weight at a discount and from overcharging the Johns because they would pay it, plus on top of all the money I was bringing in I was hooking up with all these sexy ass college girls that were paying their way through school by being smart and making dudes pay to sleep with them instead of sleeping around with everyone at school for free like all the rest of the girls in college.

Having spent most of his time hustling in Kensington, what is known to be America's largest open air drug and prostitution market, Sam was no stranger to the sex business. It was normal on the block for dealers to trade drugs with girls in exchange for sex and other sexual favors. Though from his perspective where all the girls working on the Kensington avenue strip readily trade sex for drugs and provide services for typically under $100 and then turn right around and spend it all on more drugs, Sam never thought it to be a big money-making business. Of course, unless you were a drug dealer who seemed to benefit the most from the whole situation.

Now seeing it firsthand, how a real escort service was ran and how much money the girls were making off of each client, Sam couldn't believe it. He wanted to run back to Kensington, gather all the girls off the street and put together his own operation right in Kensington, but thought better of it. Instead Sam bided his time and continued driving for the service all while learning the ins and outs of running the business.

"As I sat back and watched how my boy ran it, I quickly realized his mistakes. He was a great drug dealer, but a terrible businessman. He ran it like a drug ring, rather than a prostitution ring. He gave all the girls control over setting up their own dates and finding their own clients, and because of it he never knew how much money any of them were really earning leaving himself open to getting shortchanged regularly. It needed to be ran not like a criminal venture, but as a legitimate business, with schedules, a manager, designated girls who's only job was to set up the dates and dispatch the drivers for all the girls on shift, drivers who understood their exact roles, and then there would be no way for the girls or drivers to go rouge and steal money or get over. It was so obvious to me, but then again I've always been a better entrepreneur and businessman than I ever was a drug dealer.

Sam eventually decided to quit driving and go out and start up his own escort service, one which would rival his friends. Before leaving Sam took the opportunity to get a head start and convinced a few of the top girls who he regularly drove and had become good friends with to quit working for the service and come with him to start their own – bigger and better – service.

"I walked away from being a driver for my boy knowing that I was about to do big things. I hadn't felt that kind of rush and excitement since the afterhours spot I had blew up the way it did and became so popular. I started with just three girls, Catalina, Samantha, and Rachel. They weren't just escorts who worked for me, they were my friends and who would later become my partners in the venture. Admittedly I likely never would've been able to build it up to where it became one of the most popular services not only in Philly, but in South Jersey too. If it hadn't been for the help of those three girls. Within a matter of months we had close to twenty girls and four locations. In our first year all four of us were millionaires."

But, like all "good" things in Sam's life, the escort venture that he built into a large and lucrative criminal enterprise would not last. And just as he had with every one of his other ventures, his club, the rental scam, he made it too big not to attract unwanted attention. However, the downfall of Sam's enterprise came from the most unexpecting of places, one that no one would see coming. Sam would go on to run his escort service for almost two years before it would all come crashing down, all because of one girl from Duluth.

What made Sam's service so popular was that he

understood the key to having the best escort service was always providing the clients with a fresh variety of beautiful girls. In Sam's own words: "business is business regardless what you're selling and in the same respect consumers are all the same regardless what they're buying. A good example of this is, take an iPhone and a prostitute. Probably the two most opposite of things people buy, right? Wrong. Just how everyone wants the newest fresh iPhone every time a new model comes out, even though in reality it's basically the same as the previous older iPhone and does exactly the same things, but because it has a fresh design they'll spend hundreds of dollars more to buy it anyways. That's basic consumerism lol, and the same applies to everyone seeking out a prostitute. They all do the same things, provide the same services, but clients always want someone new, you may have the baddest escort in the city working for you, but clients who already had her would spend even more money on a girl who isn't as sexy just because she's "someone new."

Because of this, Sam spent most of his time searching for new girls to work for him, so he could continue to provide his clients with the best new girls of any of the other services in the city. Eventually, Sam began searching outside the city and hiring girls from smaller towns. It proved to be the solution to keep up with the constant high demand for new girls. And that's how Sam had found Emily, the small town girl from Duluth.

"I had no picks when it came to recruiting girls. I would go to bars, strip clubs, colleges, other services, the hood, but my favorite was online, specifically the escort ads on craigslist.com, remember this was back in 2010 before backpage.com really took off. I stopped searching in the city and started searching for girls posting ads in other areas. That's how I found Emily. She was surprisingly one of the hottest girls I had ever seen, and not just off of Craigslist, but ever in my life. So, of course I was shocked to see her ad, and even more so once I read the ad and saw she was clearly new to the game and was selling herself for far too cheap. I knew immediately that I had to have her. I was determined to bring her to Philly."

Sam contacted Emily and after several weeks of talking, he successfully convinced her to take a bus down to Philadelphia to spend a weekend with him. As he had hoped, having taken a gamble with blindly bringing an escort off of Craigslist from a different state, the beautiful girl from Duluth was real and even more attractive in person.

They both connected with each other over the course of the weekend. So much so that when it was time for Emily to catch her bus back home on Monday she ended up deciding to Stay and move in with Sam instead. What had originally supposed to be a simple offer to come down to Philly and work for him turned out to be a much more complicated situation for Sam. He unexpectedly caught feelings for the small town girl and broke his own rule he abided to ever since starting his enterprise which was to not fraternize with the girls working for him.

Even though Emily technically wasn't at that point, she eventually would be, and moved her into his condo with the intentions of having her as his girlfriend. He took care of her for about a month before he brought her into his service and had her start working for him all the while living with him still his girl.

Emily immediately caused problems among the other girls by becoming the most sought after by the clients. She worked all of two weeks before getting caught up in a hotel sting operation and arrested. For reasons unbeknownst to Sam, still to this day, the small town girl from Duluth, instead of following Sam's instructions he had embedded into her not to talk to the police and call him as soon as she was able so he could arrange to bail her out, she flipped on him, giving up everything she knew about Sam's operation.

"I had no idea Emily got arrested, when she didn't come back I just assumed she was like so many other girls who had thought they could do it, wanted to do it because how great the money was, but ultimately they just weren't able to do it.

And because of it she left to go back home without telling me. In this business that's a common occurrence, the turnover rate for the girls is like 90% in their first couple months.

This wasn't a law and order episode; I didn't have cops on the payroll or a mole in the DA's office to pass on information to me. I'll admit, it was pure dumb luck I wasn't arrested in the police raid. I had took a couple girls on a trip to Atlantic City for the weekend, who would've guessed AC of all places would be my saving grace. Once I learned of the raid and the charges against me I knew my life from that point forward would get a lot more complicated.

If the long list of charges I was facing for running the escort service and human trafficking wasn't already bad enough, I had a whole other case with even more charges because of Emily and what all that she had said about me in her statement.

And that's what I've never been able to understand with the whole situation surrounding her arrest. We were good, better than good for real, our relationship was solid, at least as solid as one could be considering the circumstances. She certainly didn't seem off in any way, even after she started working nothing changed between us. Plus, she knew – because I had made it clear – that she didn't have to work and could just live with me and be my girl. And part of me wanted her to do just that, but it was Emily who wanted to work and learn the business. She had it in her head once she learned everything that eventually she would become my partner and we'd run it together. That's why I can't figure out why she would have flipped on me so easily and completely ruin my life. Even though deep down I know it never really was her, it was the detectives playing dirty, just as they usually do, who coerced her into making up all that shit she said in her statement, so they could hit me with even more charges.

Sam returned to Philadelphia for just long enough to pack and collect his money. Panicked and unsure what to do he decided to get away from the east coast altogether and fled to Idaho to escape the heat. Once safely across the country in Idaho, back in the state where he had graduated high school at North Woods, Sam decided his life needed some new direction and he enrolled himself into college.

Giving his circumstances and wanted status back east, a more forward-thinking man might've laid low for a while, but after starting at his new school, it wasn't long before Sam was bored of normal life as a college student and saw an opportunity to get back in the game, by becoming the go-to drug dealer on campus. Needless to say, after only a couple short months, Sam was kicked out of school, the college administrators apparently frowning upon his unique brand of entrepreneurial spirit.

With nowhere to go, and not wanting to risk going back to Philadelphia, Sam would bounce around a few different midwestern states before he landed a job in Williston, North Dakota working for an oil company. All in all, it was a great job, and an even better opportunity at a better life for Sam who was regularly making over $5,000 a week as an entry level roustabout doing the hardest and dirtiest jobs on site. He did that for an entire winter before getting promoted, where he earned a permanent place in the company and an even larger salary.

Sam was enjoying his new legitimate life in North Dakota, believing his legal troubles back home were no longer an issue as long as he never returned, which he had no desire to do anyways. But, once again, like all good things in Sam's life, his new found success as a legit working class man would not last. And it would all come to an abrupt end for him one night when he was pulled over for a routine traffic stop. That night he was arrested on a fugitive of justice warrant and after a short stint in the county jail would be extradited back to Philadelphia on a commercial flight.

"I'll never forget that experience, walking onto the plane in leg shackles and handcuffs and seeing the expressions from all the passengers when they saw me, I won't lie, I got a real kick out of that – I doubt I'll ever forget it. It was priceless. It was a once in a lifetime experience, one I never would've thought to put on my bucket list, but now can add and mark it off."

Once Sam was returned to the custody of authorities in Philadelphia, a lengthy legal battle would play out. Sam was tagged by investigators as the head of the whole trafficking operation. But, with the help of his legal team, he was able to fight through many of the more serious charges.

Fortunately for Sam his lawyer was not only able to get the trafficking charges dropped, but was able to negotiate a good plea deal, which Sam took unwilling to risk taking the case to trial and potentially losing and getting sentenced to the maximum amount of time. So in 2012 at the age of only 20 Sam experienced state prison for the very first time. Then in 2014, after serving two years he was released on parole and returned to Philadelphia.

Although Sam may have been a little older and stronger both mentally and physically, he came out of prison very much the same person he had been when he went in. Nothing had changed, because of that it wasn't long before he fell right back into the criminal lifestyle. As soon as Sam reconnected with his old friends from Kensington he began using again, hustling, and knowing all too well it was only a matter of time before his parole officer caught him and sent him back to prison, he stopped reporting and went on the run.

Once again Sam became caught up in the fast criminal life in Philadelphia. The very life that he had become so addicted to before which had ultimately cost him years of his freedom. One in which he was able to do whatever he wanted without any regard for the consequences, where he could use drugs to escape having to deal with the challenges and responsibilities of the real world, and sleep around with girls and commit crimes to distract himself from all of his problems and insecurities by affording all the finer things and lavish baller lifestyle that money can buy. And of course above all else fund his expensive and excessive drug habit which extended to all of the so-called friends that he surrounded himself with.

Having come from prison and jumped right back into his old life, Sam was caught up in a continuous and dangerous cycle. One that which only ends with him either dead or getting caught, arrested, sent back to prison where the vicious cycle then repeats itself all over again and again.

"As much as I would like to be able to honestly tell you that I've finally broken the cycle and got my shit together, and my life on the right track, I can't because I am once again back in prison. This time for six years for having pulled some crazy Grand Theft Auto video game type shit while I was high on meth. I want to say that this will be it, that I am going to change

188

and live a better life once I get released from prison this time, and I'd even genuinely mean it having done quite a bit of changing and self-improving already, and having been able to accomplish so much this time in prison.

However, despite all the good that I've done over the past years while incarcerated, all the changes and self-improvements I've made, books I've written and published, Company I've started, money I've earned, People I've helped, I am still Just as I've always been - very much my own worst enemy. And I still struggle with my addiction, even now, with almost two years sober, I catch myself thinking about how much I actually miss getting high and how sometimes I want to start using again as soon as I get out, despite the fact that I know all too well if I do where that road will ultimately lead me.

And that makes me question my sobriety and its authenticity If there was meth, or even coke available in the prison, would I still have two years clean? And what if I answer no, what does that say about my chances of actually staying sober when I do return back to the streets and have the means to easily get whatever drugs I want. Not very good... That plus, I still continue to have impulsive tendencies and as much as I work on trying not to, I still seek out instant gratification even now while I'm in prison.

I know from many years of experience as a number in the DOC just how little prison actually helps you better yourself and more importantly how little it is designed to prepare you for when you're paroled or if you max out released back into society, especially after years of being incarcerated and likely institutionalized to some extent. Because of this very few inmates people come out of prison and successfully land on their feet. Most come out and quickly fall right on their ass!

And unless you put the extra time and effort into seeking out ways to help improve yourself while doing your time, prison will just be a never-ending loop of mindless unproductive bullshit over and over again for your entire sentence. And if that's how you choose to do your bid, then when the day comes that you're finally getting released and you return home you'll be blind-sided by reality. Because you'll be completely unprepared to deal with all the challenges that you undoubtedly be faced with on your first day out. And don't expect for anyone on the inside to help you by telling you what to expect once you're out, or how to handle it. They'll just release you without even giving a shit about what happens to you once you walk out the gates.

I wish that I had a book like this back when I was doing my first bid. It would've been such a game changer. Because even with family support and money, re-entry was such a challenge. From struggling to find a place to live, a job, applying for government assistance (which I didn't even know such programs were available for months because no one bothered to tell me), figuring out transportation, all the way down to relatively basic tasks, that as someone who's just spent years incarcerated can easily be challenging, like getting a cell phone, buying clothes, furniture for your new place, and every other thing that needed to be done all within the first few days of me being back home!

That is why I wanted to write this series of critically important guides for prisoners, parolees, and ex-offenders. Unlike most every other book that's been written for people like you and I, by authors who've never been in your shoes before and only think they know what they're talking about. My books come from a Place that you can actually relate too. Most importantly you will be able to learn just as much from all my failures and mistakes as you will from my proven game plans, insight, and knowledge.

I know what you really need in order to find success in prison and make your transition from prison back to the streets as easy and smooth as possible. Because of that, this book isn't just a bunch of worn-out advice, generic lessons, or bullshit resources found in most prisoner and ex-offender self-help books. I include real and important information that you'll need – just as I did – to become financially independent and successful. My game plans are full of game-changing lessons, all of which no other books, prison counselors, or really anyone for that matter, will ever bother telling you. And that's why I named my book series. The shit prisoners need to know. Because rightfully everything that I put you on to in my books is shit you need to know."

Today, Sam has left his past behind him and has an entirely new life with loftier ambitions for his future. When he returns back into society he is chasing after while he is still inside. Because of what he's been through, his first goal. It is to help others just like him in prison by fighting to bring about well overdue and much needed change to the system. In his institution and among his fellow prisoners, Sam is known as what is commonly referred to as a jailhouse lawyer., someone that is highly respected by inmates and prison staff alike., who is knowledgeable and well read on many subjects such as business, prisoner rights, and especially all things pertaining to the law. While at his institution, he has assisted others with their legal issues as well as any other types of challenges they may be facing while going through and beyond their incarceration. Sam is best known for his. Common sense from his ongoing efforts to reform Pennsylvania's Act 84. Recently, he won his lengthy legal battle with the Department of Corrections to stop them from unlawfully deducting 25 percent of all his money for court costs, fines, and restitution. Without having the necessary court order authorizing the Act 84 deductions from his inmate trust account. This action successfully paves the way for other prisoners to file a suit, and fight against the prison and win.

After the motions he filed were granted by the courts and the deductions to his money stopped, Sam, being the entrepreneur there he is, saw an opportunity to help prisoners all the while earning money. This sparked the idea for him to create his very first publication, a small thirty page booklet titled "Stopping the prisons from taking your money," which he sold to prisoners across Pennsylvania.

Sam, by way of this small book, helped hundreds of inmates with their motions and providing them with a legal guide with everything they need to know to stop the unlawful deductions of money by the prison. In return, the Department of Corrections banned his book from all Pennsylvania State correctional facilities, citing that it encouraged prisoners to circumvent legal obligations. The powers to be, clearly were not happy with the information Sam was distributing, and the increasing scrutiny that was coming over them from it. This action, however, did not have the intended effect that they had hoped it would have. Instead of discouraging Sam, it did just the opposite, motivating him that much more to further pursue his desire to create a platform to share his knowledge that is vital to the success and well-being of prisoners, parolees, and ex-offenders, not only in Pennsylvania, but across the country.

Sam pledges through his platform, to continue empowering prisoners in every way that he can providing information that they don't want you to know, sharing his knowledge to improve their lives, both inside and out of prison and most importantly, advocate for all of those who are incarcerated and fight against the violation of rights, abuse of power, and push the relevant issues with the Department of Corrections and the Criminal Justice system.

In addition to managing his publishing company and writing books from his prison cell, Sam keeps himself active throughout his institution by providing legal assistance to those who need it running workshops for aspiring and incarcerated entrepreneurs and authors, and teaching his own financial education class where he provides inmates were the important fundamentals of credit, banking, budgeting, and investing. Sam is a beacon of hope to all prisoners and ex-offenders who aspire to become successful and furthermore Is proof that with the right knowledge, mindset, and determination, you can achieve wealth and success even in the least likely of places, under the worst possible circumstances.

Upon his release from prison in 2028, Sam has big plans for his and company's future, including further expanding the reach of his educational platform. Through his company, he plans to create opportunities for incarcerated entrepreneurs and authors to become successful, not only while in prison, but out in the world as well. Sam has moved away from his old life and has achieved incredible success for himself since being incarcerated. He now looks forward to getting out for the very last time, finding the right women to start a family with and settle down to enjoy his new life. This is something he never thought possible due to the dangerous and unpredictable lifestyle he had lived for most of his life.

CONTACT US

CONTACT THE PRISONER PRESS

THE PRISONER PRESS

P.O. BOX 6053

CLEARWATER, FL 33758

Find the newest releases, book deals, information, and more at:

www.theprisonerpress.com

CONTACT AUTHOR SAM FERRARO

Write him at:

SAMUEL FERRARO #QP4526

SMART COMMUNICATION/PADOC

P.O. BOX 33028

ST. PETERSBURG, FL 33733

Email him at:

samf@theprisonerpress.com

Direct message him at:

www.connectnetwork.com

Go on to the website and set up an e-mail account to connect directly with Sam. Click "Pennsylvania Department of

Corrections." Search "Samuel Ferraro" or by his institutional number "QP4526." And then fill out your e-mail address and finish setting up your account. Once complete, you'll be able to send a direct message to Sam's tablet.

About the Series

When I first came up with the idea of creating a series of books that would help prisoners and ex-offenders with a variety of useful and important things that they need to know while in prison and once they're back out on the streets, it was just another project to keep me busy. I honestly never expected it to ever go any further than the inside of one of my record center boxes under the bunk where all my artwork, poems, and other projects end up once I'm done with them. As an inmate myself who's disconnected and cut off from the outside world with only limited communication to friends and loved ones, I understand that there is so much information and resources available that could significantly help to improve prisoners' lives while they're doing their time in prison that they simply have no way of knowing even exists, and those who do know won't ever tell "us" about it.

That's how I came up with the name THE SHIT PRISONERS NEED TO KNOW, a true-enough title that every one of "us," whether you're a prisoner or an ex-offender, can relate to. I had naturally assumed that there were hundreds of similar kinds of helpful resource books available for prisoners. My first step was to size up the competition. No reason to even start the project if there were already an abundance of books out there just like mine on the off chance that I did end up wanting to publish it, so I reached out to my people for help looking up all the current prisoner help and ex-offender re-entry books available online. Being in prison, we are restricted from using the Internet for any reason, even though many of us actually have legitimate needs for accessing the Internet, such as researching legal, business, and other just as important information that we need, like looking for housing, employment, and applying for benefits before getting released.

I was really shocked at just how few there were of up-to-date books for prisoners. Most of them were old and outdated, written years before the pandemic. Although I knew that between Amazon and Google, if a book exists, they would definitely be able to find it. Still, I couldn't believe that there weren't more current prisoner resource books, especially regarding finances, credit and money, re-entry, housing, and employment, so I signed up for the library to do my own search. I figured that if any place would have the most up-to-date collection of books for prisoners, it would be a prison library. But after searching through the entire book catalog on the library computer and coming up with nothing but even more out-of-date books, some even written as far back as the '80s and '90s, I realized right then and there that my idea of creating a series of how-to guides and resource directories for prisoners and ex-offenders was no longer just going to be another project that ends up in a box.

I knew that there was a real need for all the books I planned to write in the series. So far, there are a total of four books planned for the series, with the first book published, the second one out now, and the third in the works right now. It was one of those rare "if you build it, they will come" kind of moment for me. I knew that I needed to create this series and write books that as a prisoner I would want to read and that would help benefit me — books with relevant articles, how-to guides, and up-to-date information and resources about the real things that would benefit and help prisoners that otherwise most wouldn't to be able to find on their own.

Every book in the series is important in its own way, but my first book, The National Pro Bono Attorney Directory, is all around the most important book for everyone, not just felons or ex-offenders who are struggling to find legal aid to get their life where they want it to be. What puts every book I write on a level of its own, way above the rest, isn't just because there aren't many books out there right now that can actually compete with me that are simply much better than the few current books that are out there. It's because you know everything in my books can be trusted to be accurate, and everything I speak on I've either been through or have done myself probably more than just one occasion.

My books aren't just general how-to's on how to do this kind of book or just a bunch of facts, information, and resources, although, yeah, most of them do have a lot of that stuff inside. They also have me, and, more importantly, my own personal knowledge, experience, including my successes and failures, mistakes, insights, and all the things in life that I know so much about. Who knew that being a "bad guy" living the criminal fast lifestyle would actually one day benefit not only me but many others who want to make a legitimate way, that all my insider knowledge over a decade's worth of real life experience dealing with and being exposed to the American Criminal Justice System, Department of Corrections and parole boards would be used to help those inside persons, parolees, ex-offenders, and addicts better themselves and find their way to the outside world and become successful once they are released and back on the street.

When I was researching other books similar to the one I wanted to write for the series, besides discovering there weren't nearly enough of them, I was just as surprised to see that every ex-offender re-entry and prison help book I found was written by just about every other type of person except for the one type who actually should write them, which is those who actually have been in those shoes of the people that these books are supposed to help, parolees, and ex-offenders. I couldn't believe out of all the books, not one single author was an ex-offender themselves! It's like they want to teach all these "normal" people who really don't know shit about what it's like being a prisoner or an ex-offender are profiting off people like you and me.

They write books explaining how to make it in the world on parole and as an ex-offender when they themselves have likely never even been arrested, let alone experience what it's really like to return to society after having been locked away in prison for years. They can't truly relate or even understand the psychological shock and difficulty it is for an ex-offender to try and process the sudden change from waking up in prison to a few hours later being released and right back on the streets, all the while having to deal with the enormous challenges that come with trying to piece together an entirely new life.

Anyone can put together a book with a bunch of statistics, general re-entry information and national and state resources and call it a re-entry book. In fact, basically everyone that I've read so far is exactly that: all basic facts without any real substance from actually people like me who have been there, done it, and have the scars, emotional baggage, and prison numbers to show for it. Put it this way: If my professional resume was anywhere near as extensive and accomplished as my criminal resume is, I'd pretty much be able to land a top position at any Fortune 500 company that I wanted, making billions of dollars a year. Unfortunately, my criminal experience doesn't transfer over to professional experience, but it does make me the most qualified to write about all my experiences in having gone through all of the various levels as a repeat "client" of the American Criminal Justice System, Incorporated, and its subsidiary company, The Department of Corrections.

I wrote this book, not because I wanted to cash out from writing about my own personal experiences as both a criminal and state inmate or to create a new, popular trending prisoner book series for profit. Contrary to what you might think, you don't get rich off writing these types of non-fiction books, especially when you're doing everything from your prison cell like I am. Unlike the rest of the authors, I've been about that life and know how hard it can be to do time, to make parole, to get out and have to start all over again with nothing, and I certainly understand all too well how challenging it can be to find good legal aid, especially if you can't afford to hire an attorney.

I've been locked up in nine different county jails and seven state prisons. Admittedly, so far, every time that I've returned back into the community from prison, I've never actually succeeded in my re-entry journey. But yet, here I am writing an entire series of books on, among other things, helping you succeed at re-entry. I might have never been able to succeed myself, but I know what it takes. And besides, if you learn anything from my experience, it certainly will be what not to do when you get out. That's my real motivation behind writing this book and every other book in the series—to help you become the best version of yourself by sharing my knowledge and insight and also by learning from all of my epic mistakes to not be like me but be better than me.

Thanks for Your Interest in The Prisoner Press.

We value our customers and would like to hear from you!

We strive for the best, so reviews are an important tool in bringing you quality publications. We want to know our readers' opinions on whether you think it's good or not.

If you could take the time to review/rate any of the publications you've read from The Prisoner Press, we would appreciate it. If your loved ones use Amazon, have them post your review on the books you've read, and using Amazon's five-star rating system, post your rating. This will help us tremendously in providing future publications that are even more useful and informative to our readers and growing our business.